John Gierach

ILLUSTRATED
BY GLENN WOLFF

Standing in a River Waving a Stick

SIMON & SCHUSTER

SIMON & SCHUSTER

Rockefeller Center

1230 Avenue of the Americas

New York, NY 10020

Copyright © 1999 by John Gierach

All rights reserved, including the right of reproduction
in whole or in part in any form.

SIMON & SCHUSTER and colophon are registered trademarks
of Simon & Schuster Inc.

Briefer versions of these stories first appeared in Fly Rod & Reel, Outdoor
Life, Field & Stream, Big Sky Journal, and Sports Afield.

Designed by Karolina Harris

Manufactured in the United States of America

10 9 8 7 6 5 4 3 2 1

Library of Congress Cataloging-in-Publication Data

Gierach, John, date.

Standing in a river waving a stick / John Gierach : illustrated by Glenn Wolff.

p.   cm.

1. Fly fishing—North America—Anecdotes. I. Title.

SH462.G54   1999

799.1'24'097—dc21   98-43853

CIP

ISBN 0-684-82425-6

Contents

Contents

Standing
in a River
Waving a Stick

———————

The doctor told how he was once fishing in the Wind River area of Wyoming and he looked up and far above on the side of the canyon two dogs sat on a rock peeking at him from the brush that surrounded the rock. Only they weren't dogs, they were coyotes. They were curious about what he might be doing standing in a river waving a stick.

—JIM HARRISON
Farmer

Chapter 1

The Happy Idiot

LATELY I've been thinking about what makes a good fly-fisher, possibly the last fair question of the twentieth century that might actually have an answer. I mean that in a purely technical sense, as in someone who's pretty good at catching fish on a fly rod. The other stuff—the humor, graciousness, inner peace or whatever—is important and may even turn out to be the whole point, but I'm not sure you can learn that part. I'm beginning to think it either comes by itself with time, or not.

On the other hand, I think you *can* learn to be a good fisherman (at least I hope so), and it's probably easier to get all philosophical about it when you actually catch some fish now and then.

The best way to pick up the nuts and bolts of something like fly-fishing has always been face to face with someone who already knows—whether it's a teacher, a friend or a kindly stranger—and there can be a lot to learn. Twenty or thirty years ago, when it was becoming fashionable for fishermen to use the Latin names for bugs, outdoor writers joked about getting a doctoral degree in fly-fishing. Now, with introductory to advanced classes, seminars, demonstrations, books and videos on everything from casting to fly tying, certification of casting instructors and such, you can damn near do that, although how much study you need before you're qualified to hook and land a fish is still an open question.

In fact, there are times when fly-fishing seems to be suffering from the same malady that afflicts the rest of society: too many so-called facts and not enough real experience, but I have to say the quality of information on fly-fishing is better than most. Sure, there's the normal showmanship, bullshit or whatever else you want to call it, but if you do precisely what a magazine article tells you to do in the exact conditions described, you'll probably catch some fish. On the other hand, you could also catch fish by doing something completely different. Maybe even bigger ones, or more of them.

Not long ago one of those prime-time TV news shows followed the performance of two stock portfolios, one picked by a heavyweight investment counselor, the other picked by a monkey. Naturally, the monkey won. (The investment guy took it well. He said, "Can I have the monkey's phone number?") Fly-fishing can be like that, too. You'll probably do well going by the book, but there's also a kind of random goofiness in operation that rewards the happy idiot.

It would be handy to put together the kind of profile the FBI assembles on mad bombers—"your typical good fly-fisher is a single, middle-aged male of moderate to low intelligence, sullen, withdrawn, probably lives with his mother"—but actually, all the really good fly-fishers I know are unique.

If one is a real match, the hatch-style technician who counts the tails on mayflies and fishes flawless, entomologically correct imitations, another will catch just as many trout drifting a Royal Wulff through the same hatch. For everyone who fishes hard from an hour before dawn until midnight, someone else will land just as many fish but still somehow manage to spend half the day sleeping under a tree.

It *is* true that most good fly-fishers can go through the motions reasonably well. They can cast, wade, find and stalk fish, select fly patterns, tie strong knots and all that, but if one is the kind of person who'd naturally become a great caster, then that's how he comes at it. If not, maybe he becomes an adventurous wader to make up for it, slogging to within fifteen feet of the spot someone else will cast all the way across the river to reach. It's rare for even the best fishermen to be experts at everything, but one way or another, they all get the fly to the fish.

And things change over time, too. I'll probably never be a truly great fly caster, but I'm better than I used to be, I do work at it and there have been a few fish I've caught only because I managed to make a great throw. But then I've only gotten to be a progressively better caster as my trick knee has gotten trickier (it's been known to pop out of joint when pushed sideways by a strong current). I guess I'm just taking up slack, although I prefer to think of it as systematically replacing the brute force of youth with adult finesse.

Then again, even though I do cast a little better, I can still get around in the water well enough, too. Years of extreme wading taught me how to pick easier routes through bad currents, and I've actually developed a meditation technique that lets me lower my center of gravity when I'm in the water. So maybe you can do a little better than just break even. With luck, it can be like quitting drinking without entirely losing the sense of fun you learned while you were smashed.

I've also noticed that a lot of good fishermen have the uncanny ability to immediately turn any conversation to angling with a fly rod, on the theory that the essence of anything is in how it's either like or unlike fishing, and they often do it so deftly they don't even stretch the point.

My friend Pat Leonard is in the music business and he's pretty successful at it. (Many good fly-fishers also seem to be very good at something else, too. I'm not sure why, although I have some half-baked ideas.) Anyway, it's become kind of a joke with us to crack any subject by pretending to search for just the right analogy and then finally saying, "Well, it's sort of like fishing, isn't it?"

The other day Pat was talking about the agonies of writing music, I said, "So it's sort of like fishing, then," and he said, "Well, yeah, except on a bad day your piano doesn't swim under a rock and stay there until you go away."

Pat's real successful, as I said, but after too many years spent as a trout bum, I can't help thinking of him as a fisherman who works part-time as a famous record producer to support his habit. Then again, he's enough of a fisherman that he might agree with me.

I also have to say that the best fishermen I know are fanatics—although most have been that way for so long that a kind of eerie calm has settled over them, so it's not always obvious—and they also spend a hell of a lot of time fishing. Some can do that because they have a lot of money. Others don't have much money because they spend a hell of a lot of time fishing. It's like getting the fly to the fish: one way or another, they get it done.

That's probably the most important part of getting really good at this. Tom McGuane once wrote, "Angling is extremely time consuming. That's sort of the whole point," and it's occurred to me a few times, when I've gotten into some local political battle or idly wondered how I'd be paying the mortgage in the next ten or twenty years, that God must have invented fly-fishing to keep old hippies from getting rich or ruling the world.

But then some of us who have it bad for fishing either don't hanker that much for money and power or don't care to do what it takes to get them. All we really want is bigger trout, better rods and a happy sex life.

I guess the one thing all great fly-fishers have in common is, they seem to have figured something out that's eluded the rest of us. Spend much time around one of these guys and you begin to suspect that whatever it takes to catch fish, it's not quite what you thought it was. But the hidden truth behind that is, it took them years on the water to arrive at it. It's not just fishing, either. Ask anyone you know who's very good at anything if there's a shortcut to spending half a lifetime learning the ropes and letting something indefinable slowly sink in.

Of course the hidden truth behind *that* is, just putting in the time is no guarantee. You also have to have passion and curiosity and then learn how to satisfy both, but at the same time not take it too seriously. I've been known to get downright mystical about fly-fishing, and I really do believe that you're as likely to find the meaning of life in catching fish as anywhere else, but I've also learned that spiritual quests can be disappointing, as when you go off to search for your spirit animal, only to find that it's a bunny rabbit.

It's probably better to just do the thing because it seems

worth doing for its own sake, and if something more comes of it along the way, fine. Some of the best fishermen I know really want to catch fish, can be disappointed when things go badly and have an ego, a competitive streak, and all the other regulation human failings, but most days they seem to fish the way a dog follows its master: with nothing much in mind except to see what's gonna happen next.

Over the years I've been lucky enough to have fished with a precious handful of great fly-fishers: people who could catch at least some fish when no one else could get a strike, or who caught more and bigger fish when everyone else was getting their share, who did that on a pretty regular basis, who seemed to do it almost effortlessly and who usually didn't brag or strut or otherwise beat you over the head with their success.

It seems like I've spent a lot of time trying to copy what better fly-fishers were doing, and it's surprising how often that hasn't worked. You know the drill: Your partner is just hammering fish. He generously gives you the secret fly pattern, he tells you what size tippet he's using and what kind of drift he's trying for, maybe he even trades spots with you. He continues to hammer fish. You still can't buy a strike, and his kindness only makes you feel more dimwitted than you felt before.

So what the hell has he got that you don't? Whatever it is, it's just too elusive. You can't steal it, and he can't give it away. The more you watch him, the more he seems to just be letting it happen instead of making it happen (the smug bastard), but when *you* try to just let it happen, it doesn't. If you come right out and ask him what he's doing, he'll either say he doesn't know himself, or he'll tell you something too simple and obvious to be of any use. (Spencer Tracy once said the secret to acting is "Learn the lines and don't bump into the furniture.")

Still, I think I've learned from these guys. Now and then it's been something you could include in a list of A Hundred Tips for Lunker Trout—some good advice on casting, a fly pattern, a better knot—but mostly it's just the feeling that you have to come at this in your own way.

I know I'm a long way from greatness, but I *am* beginning to come at it in my own way. I can go through the basic motions pretty well, don't rely quite as religiously on specific fly patterns as I once did, have worked out ways of compensating for some of my most egregious weaknesses and have come to count heavily on timing because it's a hell of a lot easier to catch fish when the fish are biting.

I also pay close attention to small details, not because any one thing is likely to be the Big Answer but because I think if you methodically string lots of little things together and then stand back and look at the whole picture, the light will eventually begin to dawn.

But I know there's more to it—or maybe less—if only because that sounds like good advice. If I really had it, I'd be able to say something that was completely useless in a kind of Zen-like way.

But at least I share two articles of faith with the great

fishermen: I believe that the solution to any problem—work, love, money, whatever—is to go fishing, and the worse the problem, the longer the trip should be. And I'm also certain that on the day I become a truly sublime fly-fisher, all my failings will be overshadowed and all my demons will swim under rocks and stay there until I go away.

Chapter 2

A New Pond

LAST summer I had one of those chance meetings that changed the complexion of what had been shaping up as sort of a nothing day. I was sitting in Mike Clark's bamboo fly-rod shop in Lyons, Colorado, where I automatically end up around lunchtime most days when I'm in town. In fact, I'm there often enough that I have my own rocking chair. It's in a corner near the workbench, close to the stove for warmth in the winter, just as close to the back door for a breeze in summer.

I think having a reserved chair qualifies me as a bona fide regular, like having a cup with your name on it over at the coffee shop. Mike agrees, although he's more likely to call me "the king shop rat."

We'd just had lunch specials over at the Lyons Café (it was meat loaf day—a high point in the week) and we were back in the shop, drinking coffee and discussing the possibility of either getting something accomplished in our respective careers yet that day or maybe going fishing: the kind of dilemma you can hash over until it's too late to do either.

In fact, it's this tendency that has given fishermen their time-honored reputation for being lazy, but of course that's a bum rap. We're not lazy, we just don't like to rush into things.

Anyway, we'd just started speculating about the possibility of an evening hatch on the nearby St. Vrain Creek when I spotted someone across the street who looked familiar. I said to Mike, "Isn't that John Barr over there?"

Mike glanced through the front window and said, "I don't know. I never met him."

I hadn't seen John in a couple of years myself, although he lives just down the road in Boulder, but it sure looked like him from a distance, so I trotted across the street, and sure enough, when I got close he smiled and said, "Grits!"

I've known John for so many years that he's now one of

only two or three people who still call me "Grits." Never mind why.

He came back over to the shop with me and met Mike, which was fun to watch. John is a well-known fly tier, originator of—among other good patterns—the famous Barr Emerger, and Mike is also well known for his hand-made bamboo fly rods. It's interesting to watch two people meet who have known each other by reputation for a long time. It's always an "Ah, so you're him" kind of thing, and then each looks closely at the other for some physical sign of genius, even though it usually doesn't show.

John was relaxed and easygoing, as usual, and Mike was friendly and talkative that day, even though he has a reputation among local fishermen for being kind of grumpy. I think it's mostly an act, although he has some people pretty well convinced. Someone once said of him, "Beneath that gruff exterior beats the heart of a real son of a bitch."

We looked at some rods (all good-looking fly rods must be put together and wiggled, even though few of us can tell much about a rod without a line on it), and then we got to talking about fishing. We all agreed that the trout fishing had been a little slow so far this year, with the high water and all, and John said he'd been fishing almost exclusively for bass and panfish.

We asked him where—the question you always ask, fully expecting a "Here and there" kind of answer but hoping, too, that the guy will drop a great hint.

John said he had access to a nice warm-water pond and

told us a little bit about it in the way an honest fisherman will: in general terms first (it has nice fish, but not *huge* fish) and then in terms of the three or four biggest fish ever caught there, just so you understand that it may not be the cosmic honey hole or anything but still has the appropriate aura of mystery about it. Then he said, casually, "You guys want to fish it?"

"When?" we asked.

"Now," he said.

"Okay."

There was a flurry of activity then—the kind of mild panic you see in a couple of fishermen who might have spent the afternoon goofing off but who are now actually going fishing. I had to blast home, grab a rod and vest and quickly switch my trout-fly boxes for my bass and bluegill boxes. It took about five minutes, including a few seconds to wonder why the same chore can take me three hours when I have more warning.

In a few minutes Mike had turned the sign in his shop window from OPEN to GONE FISHING and we were in my pickup following John's Jeep south out of town, each hoping we hadn't forgotten anything crucial. I was trying to remember if I'd brought my reel. Mike said, "I don't *think* I have any appointments this afternoon. . . . "

Twenty minutes later we turned off a paved county road in front of an old but well-kept farmhouse, went down a narrow dirt track and came to a locked gate. John got out to work the combination on the lock, and Mike got out to close the gate behind both vehicles.

This has always been one of my favorite moments in fishing: following the kindly angler through the locked gate and down to the new pond. I've done it often, and it usually goes well enough; there are some fish, a few get caught. On certain rare occasions the pond turns out to be a pitiful mud hole with no signs of life, and at other, just as rare times, it turns out to be the best fishing I've had in the last five years. But whatever happens, those last few minutes, as you follow your host's vehicle down the last stretch of dirt road, straining for the blue flash of water through the trees, are pregnant with suspense.

I've been fishing around the county for a long time, but this was a pond I'd never gotten on before. Mike has fished more ponds around here than I have, and since he was in the excavating business before he started making bamboo fly rods for a living, he actually built a lot of them. But this was a new one to him, too. Proving that life, even around home, can still be an adventure.

I said, "I didn't even know there was a pond back here."

Mike said, "*I* did."

It was a pretty pond; once a gravel pit, probably, but old enough now that you'd have to look hard to see that it was anything but a small, natural lake with a little marsh on one side. I'll guess it at ten or fifteen acres, although I'm not good at judging surface area. About half of it looked shallow enough to wade, with cattails along one side and sprawling, broken weed beds opening out onto a big patch of open water that would be the deep end.

We stopped on the grassy patch where others had apparently parked their cars, though not a lot of others by the look of it. There were the broken stretches of tall weeds, wooden fence posts trailing sagging barbed wire and suckering Russian olives you'll see on a place that hasn't been farmed or grazed for a while. The horizon in every direction was hemmed in with tall, old, river-bottom cottonwood trees, which is why I'd never spotted the pond from the road.

It was a warm afternoon a few weeks into June, with a blue sky, puffy white cumulus clouds and just enough of a breeze to ruffle the water a little at the east end of the pond but leave the weedy end glassy. It seems to me now that there were flies buzzing, grasshoppers clicking, frogs chirping, sparrows and finches twittering, something— probably little sunfish—plopping in the water: the kind of summer pond noises you almost don't hear but that you'd miss if they stopped.

A few panfish swirled out on the water, and at least one decent-looking bass boiled in a shady spot along some cattails. This was after the bass and sunfish would have spawned, so the fish were off the beds, but it wasn't yet into the dog days, when a pond can go dead through the middle of the day. It was, in fact, one of my favorite times to fish a warm-water pond: in those early warm days when the fish are prowling and hungry.

As we rigged up, John talked about the pond affectionately, pointing out sweet spots, mentioning critters he'd seen fish eat and so on—the kind of thing that, on paper, would amount to a tight, no-nonsense paragraph or two. As usual, it wasn't so much a description of the pond itself as a rough sketch of how John fishes and what kind of flies he likes—which is actually much more interesting.

I always listen carefully to whatever the guy who knows the new water wants to tell me, and I'll usually watch him fish, too. Some of the most valuable things a good fisherman knows about familiar water are so subtle they're almost impossible to communicate (which is why you can't really learn to fish from a book) or so eccentric they'll only work for that guy. Still, you watch and listen and maybe a little of it sinks in.

John tied on a big-headed, goggle-eyed, deer-hair-and-marabou thing he'd tied himself—a meat-and-potatoes fly for large bass. Mike started with a dark feather-winged streamer, and I put on a thin, size-8 cork-bodied popper with dangly rubber legs: the kind of surreal warm-water contraption that's as likely to catch a big bluegill as a bass—a fly that says, We can specialize later. Right now, let's just see what's in here.

What was in there was the usual mix of panfish we get around here. There were bluegills, bluegill/green hybrids, rock bass and the odd pumpkinseed. Most were small, a few would have been keepers, and two I caught—a bluegill and a rock bass—were big and pretty enough for me take some color pictures.

There were also quite a few chubby largemouth bass

from, say, 12 to 14 or 15 inches, and these were the mid-day, shallow-water fish that struck on or near the surface. That meant there were probably bigger ones that would sulk in deep water during the day and maybe move in the evenings or at night.

I guess a fisherman always looks at new water that way: trying to allow as much for what he doesn't see as for what he does and then making a picture based partly on faith. That's where our reputation as liars comes from. Another bum rap.

In other words, it was a workmanlike bass-and-panfish pond, like many others I've fished over the years, on a quiet, slow-paced day that was also not unlike others I've spent in the company of friends, listening to birds sing, watching shadows lengthen, catching a fish now and then and being in the one kind of place on earth where I feel like I know the score: a place where I understand enough to get in quietly and make something small but good happen, and on those days when it doesn't happen, well, that's okay, too.

I guess there was nothing special about it except that I was once again doing something I love dearly and that I get to do often. Sometimes, as I slump in my rocking chair at Mike's shop after lunch and he stands at the workbench planing bamboo, we talk about the hassles of being self-employed in obscure corners of weird businesses. We work as hard as we think we should and we do okay, al-

though we've both been told more than once that we
could do a lot better.

Once a guy actually told me that if I was smart I'd be in
L.A. writing screenplays instead of in the Colorado
foothills banging out fishing stories. Maybe he's right, although with my luck I'd end up writing *The Trout That
Ate Denver,* attending the premiere at a drive-in outside
Loose Gravel, Iowa, and missing a whole fishing season in
the process.

And anyway, Mike and I think we know the pitfalls of
all that. I mean, we've both seen people walk away from
perfectly good lives to make lots of money, only to end up
spending all that money and more trying to buy their old
lives back. It seems like a waste of time. As it is, we're
making some kind of living doing what we'd happily do
for free, and I think we both already have what most fishermen long for: lives in which, however a day begins, it
could end by bagging work to go catch a few fish, and
there's no one we have to make excuses to.

In fact, it couldn't have been three hours earlier that
Mike told me there weren't enough hours in a day to
make all the rods he had orders for, but I understood that
some of the days he was talking about would necessarily
be like this one.

John was fairly close to me when I caught that big rock
bass, so he waded over to look at it and then held it for me
while I took the photo. He said, "Hell of a fish," and then

asked to see the popper I was using. It was a store-bought job made in Akron, Ohio, so I couldn't take the credit for inventing it or even for tying it. I catch so many fish on these things that I order them by the dozen, in four different colors. John seemed to like it, so I gave him a couple. It seemed like the least I could do.

That was one time we were close enough to have much of a conversation. For most of the afternoon it was just the occasional one- or two-syllable comment: "All right," "Good," "Oops," "Shit." The one other time John and I got within speaking distance of each other I asked, just to make conversation, "So how's business?"

He said, "Thanks for reminding me."

Chapter 3

Grizzly Central

I DON'T know whether Dave Brown loves driving so much that he does it with great enthusiasm, or he hates it so much he can't wait to get where he's going so he can get out of the truck. Once I thought it was just his eagerness to fish, but then I noticed he drove every bit as hard, if not a little harder, on the way home. I guess it's just an idle question. Whatever the reason, he goes like a bat out of hell.

Anyway, last August Dave, A.K. Best, and I were barreling down an old, wet logging road in the mountains of British Columbia on our way to a cutthroat trout stream. Dave was at the wheel—holding it with both hands, thank God—and we were going faster than you'd think you'd want to through slick mud, standing puddles and jumbled rocks. We'd been barreling for an hour without seeing another vehicle or even a tire track in the mud, and as far as I could tell, we were nowhere near a river.

It was A.K.'s first trip to this part of Canada. I'd fished with Dave, a fly-fishing guide out of Calgary, Alberta, for the last few seasons, and the year before he'd brought me to this area to look at some water he thought he might like to guide clients on. Technically, it wasn't a guided trip, it was a scouting operation with an off-duty guide, which in some ways is better.

We'd found some good fishing on that previous trip, and even in somewhat civilized surroundings with fair-to-middling access, there were days when we were in the only MacKenzie boat on ten-mile stretches of river, catching native west-slope cutthroats so innocent they'd almost break your heart.

A.K. decided to come along this time after hearing my stories—which, as an old friend, he understood to be as true as could reasonably be expected—and after learning that on this trip we'd be going to a smaller, wilder, lesser-known, more remote river (name withheld by request).

Dave would only refer to the river as Grizzly Central, because it flows through a corner of B.C. that has the largest concentration of grizzly bears in the province. (Of course that's not the river's real name, but I guess it *is* your one hint if you care to pursue it.)

About an hour and a half up the old logging road—along which there'd been several opportunities to take a wrong turn and get lost—we pulled over at the forested lip of a steep gorge. It was a cool, overcast, drizzly day: no wind; tall, silent spruce/fir forest. It was so quiet I could hear a single chickadee far down the slope, and *way* down there I could just make out the faint hissing of running water.

Dave said, "So this is it."

The route down followed game trails for a while, then dropped off into thick brush and slippery mud and down slopes steep enough that it was work even with gravity in your favor. And of course after several hundred feet of this, it began to occur to you that at some point you were going to have to drag your sorry ass back out of there. We finally came to the river on the outside of a gentle bend and on the wrong side of a tremendous logjam, so that the last few yards to the water took another ten minutes to negotiate.

The river was on the small side, but still plenty big enough. There were places where you could ford it easily and other places where one bad step would float your hat: big enough to drown in but too small to be navigable (and how would you get a boat in there anyway?), although I know some serious kayakers who'd probably want to try it.

It's a glacial river, so it had that raw, dramatic, flood-blasted look to it. The rocks were clean, polished and chalky-looking, and in places the channel and banks were choked with splintered logjams—some old and bleached, some from the previous spring runoff still oozing sap and sporting green needles. The narrow banks of the river were mostly bare, with scattered driftwood and tough little clumps of juniper, but the thick, dark coniferous forest came right to the high-water line like a green wall.

The riffles and shallower runs were glass clear, but the deeper pools had that eerie, almost medicinal aquamarine cast glacial rivers get. Since the larger trout tend to pod up in the deep holes, you quickly learn to associate that color with fish.

I don't think the woods there are technically rain forest, but in places they give that impression, right down to carpets of moss and waist-high ferns. One minute you think you could hear a grizzly bear coming for half a mile in this stuff, and that's sort of comforting; the next minute you think you could step on a sleeping bear before you saw it. Whichever way you look at it, you can't help thinking of bears.

Dave wanted to fish this thing because, although it does have a reputation in certain circles, it's not well known, even locally, and it protects itself pretty well. Many of the fishermen who aren't discouraged by the long, rugged drive are turned off by the climb in and out of the place. And then others who could handle all that are scared off by the grizzly bears. (I'm not saying A.K. and I weren't scared of the bears ourselves, just that we weren't scared *off.*) The upshot is, not many people fish the river, even among those who know about it, and of course not everyone knows about it.

Dave likes to sniff out places like this because, as a guide, he wants to have a little something extra up his sleeve. If you were talking to a banker or an accountant, you could say this was about business and not be lying, although that wouldn't be the whole story, either.

For my part, some of the sweetest fly-fishing I've ever done has been in the company of guides I knew who just wanted to check out a rumor or run down a hunch and asked if I wanted to come along for grins. There have been times when it was said I was there as a kind of consultant to "help evaluate the fishery," and that, too, would have been true enough as far as it goes.

The drill on many of these British Columbia cutthroat rivers is, you fish dry flies because they're classy and because nine times out of ten they're all you need, at least in the summer and fall. The year before, on another river in the area, Dave tried a nymph because a guide needs to know what all will work, as well as just what's the most fun. He gave up on it after several fish in a row ignored his Pheasant Tail and tried to eat the strike indicator. That's one of the stories I told A.K., who is, after all, as close to being a dry-fly purist as any fisherman I know.

That was on a larger river that actually gets some fishing pressure, though not much. On the more remote streams, the cutts are even bigger suckers for dry flies, if that's possible. If there's a hatch on, you fish something roughly resembling the real bugs. If not, you try a big hopper or a stonefly.

To most of the fly-fishers I'd met in the area, a really small fly was a size 16, and exact imitation of real bugs was considered unnecessary for cutthroats, if not downright effete. The first time we'd fished over there, I had dutifully brought along my South Platte and Frying Pan River fly boxes with dozens of painstakingly tied mayflies and midges in sizes 18 through 26. Dave had shaken his head at the tininess of them, said they were real pretty and told me to leave them at home next time.

We climbed out of the logjam, waded across a shallow riffle and spread out, stepping over white driftwood and clattering through loose cobbles. Dave—always the guide, off duty or not—pointed me toward a long, deep pool and told me to try a size 8 Stimulator. On my first cast with it, I missed what looked like a 20-inch cutthroat. (I was still limbering up, catching my breath, taking in the scenery; I wasn't ready.) Dave said, matter-of-factly, "Nice fish, ey? Maybe we'll get 'im on the way back."

A few casts later I was into a smaller trout—Dave had just released one upstream from me—and downstream I could hear A.K. laughing, which meant he had one, too. A.K. has the habit of bursting out laughing when he hooks a fish, as if, after a lifetime of fly-fishing, he's still amazed that it actually works. You get used to it after a while, and if you're not careful, you'll begin to see the humor in it and start laughing yourself.

From there we leapfrogged upstream, if only because upstream always seems more adventurous than down. We went mostly from pool to pool, sometimes fishing close enough together to talk, other times wandering off out of sight alone, where I would begin to think about bears again.

I haven't fished a lot in bear country, but I've done it enough to have learned that phantom bears can be worse than real ones. On rivers in Alaska I've had brown bears stroll down to the same bank I was fishing to catch salmon, sometimes more than one adult, sometimes a sow with cubs—the most dangerous combination. It's a shock, but it can also be sort of a relief. I mean, the largest part of the mystery is solved, because *there they are!*

But not seeing them and *wondering* if they're there can gnaw at you. It's possible to hear things in the constant rushing and tumbling of a fast river. At times I've heard distinct voices speaking whole sentences, so growls, grunts and heavy footsteps aren't much of a stretch for me. And on that river in B.C. I noticed that if you glanced into the dark forest on the far bank, you could easily locate any number of large, brown things. If you looked up quickly from the stream, with the afterimage of the flowing water still working on your retinas, they could even seem to move.

You're supposed to make noise so if there *is* a bear

around, you won't surprise him. I did that, but then it occurred to me that maybe a middle-aged man in the middle of nowhere singing Grateful Dead lyrics off-key might be a little surprising in itself. As I said, it can gnaw at you. You think, Maybe it's common knowledge among grizzly bears that graying Dead Heads are delicious and easy to catch.

Some people who spend a lot of time in bear country wear bear bells on their packs or vests to alert bears to their presence. There's an old joke about that: How can you tell the droppings of black bears and grizzlies apart? The grizzly turds are the ones with the bells in them.

Fear of bears isn't something any of us had talked a lot about. A.K. had mentioned some misgivings about being on foot and unarmed in bear country—in the thin-lipped but casual way of someone who knows there's not much to discuss—and he did seem a little subdued. Me too, maybe. I've noticed that in spots like that I'm torn between wanting to make lots of noise and wanting to hold my breath and listen for the snapping of twigs.

Dave seemed completely unconcerned. Maybe he was, maybe he wasn't. Those who live and fish around bears do eventually grow a harder shell than the rest of us, and guides also know that most clients are easier to spook than high-strung racehorses, so they learn to exude a Chuck Yeager–style calm, even when things get a little tense.

The trout in that small river were all sizes, from streamlined little dinks in the pocket water to fat 16- and 18-

inchers in the pools, maybe even a few larger than that. (I want to say 20 inches because it's such a round and satisfying number, but I can't quite say it with confidence, because we didn't actually measure any fish.) They were light-colored trout, to match the bare rock bottom of the river, with pale olive backs, yellowish bellies, pinkish-orange fins, slashes and gill covers and small, black spots running high along the back and clustering toward the tail.

And they were romantic as hell, being trout that could trace their ancestry directly back to the last ice age with no interruptions, no detours through a hatchery.

They were pretty gullible, too. Even with no hatch on, they'd rocket off the bottom of a four- or five-foot-deep pool for a big dry fly without a hint of suspicion. There's a kind of fisherman who calls wild cutthroats stupid—and I guess I've said that myself a time or two, just to make the point—but really they're just unused to the idea of human fishermen, without a clue that some godawful shaving brush of a fly could be anything but a real, edible bug.

A.K. and I have talked about that. It takes time, trouble and sometimes money to get to places like this, and we do it—*when* we do it—not so much for the easy fishing as to experience that kind of innocence. Maybe we're hoping a little of it will rub off.

And I guess there's just something I like about pure-strain cutthroats, especially a race I'm not very familiar with. Before I started going to British Columbia, the only other west-slope cutts I'd ever caught were on the up-stream end of the Bitterroot River in Montana. They were smaller than the ones in B.C., and if I remember right, not as easy to catch. Some of the details of that trip have faded with time, but for some reason I distinctly remember nailing a bunch of nice ones one afternoon on size-16 Flick-style Red Quills, after being told by a local guide that all you needed to catch fish on the Bitterroot was a size-10 Ugly Radamus.

I also remember a bear story from that trip. That same week, up around Kalispell, a Fish & Wildlife guy was attacked by a grizzly he was trying to release from one of those big culvert live traps. He had to kill the bear with his revolver, and in an interview from his hospital bed he said he never heard any of the six shots, but when he ran out of bullets he distinctly heard the hammer click on the empty chamber.

By early afternoon we'd come to a place where the river leveled out a little and braided itself through an almost flat bench of sparsely wooded land. The overcast had lifted and broken enough to let shafts of sunlight down to the river, making the bleached rocks whiter and the forest darker by comparison. The trout were rising to a good hatch of little Green Drakes, or what a fly-fisher claiming to know some entomology would probably call Flavilineas.

I had some of those in my big dry-fly box, from a batch

I'd tied the previous winter. They were a little snazzier than what I usually fish—divided-wing parachutes with delicate floss ribs and split tails: the kind of fly you tie when you have time on your hands.

Effete or not, the fish liked them. I was proud of that, and even though Dave and A.K. were catching just as many on Wulffs and Humpies, I imagined that the trout ate my flies with more obvious relish.

The next morning we hiked into the same river at another spot. If anything, the climb down was longer, steeper and muddier, with looser rocks. We caught more cutthroats, about the same size range, though maybe not quite as many, and also hung a few bull trout on streamers. Some of those were 20 inches easy, fine fish, but nothing too outrageous considering that even in the smaller rivers they can grow to ten pounds on a diet consisting mostly of young cutthroats.

There are resident fly-fishers up there who specialize in bull trout and head-hunt them with size-2, lead-eyed Geek Leeches and such. They're a really cool fish, actually: chubby, moody, big, a kind of Dolly Varden, they say, although they strike me more as a cross between a lake trout and a pike. They're gray/green, faintly spotted, seriously predatory and almost monstrously out of place in a small river. They can be hard to spot because they're too big and you can mistake them for logs, but sometimes when you're playing a decent-sized cutthroat, a huge shape on the bottom comes to life and tries to kill your fish.

I hadn't forgotten about the bears, but I guess I'd re-laxed a little. If nothing else, having a full day of imagi-nary bear sightings under your belt makes you think you might just survive the whole trip—especially if you re-main vigilant.

When it comes right down to it, I've actually reached a kind of inner peace about bears. After all, I love wild places, and in North America grizzly bears are the signa-ture of wildness, so they're part of the deal. I knew that, statistically, at least, I'd be in a lot more danger on the drive back over the mountains to Alberta with Dave at the wheel, barreling through the darkness with the Mack boat fishtailing behind us on the curves. I also understood that getting killed and eaten by a large predator in—that sum-mer—the forty-eighth year of a mostly good life, would probably be a better end than most. Not that I hoped for that—far from it. I guess I just found it interesting that I could be scared shitless and happy at the same time.

By the end of that second day we'd worked our way down-stream into an enormous, mile-wide glacial moraine: an eerie landscape of polished cobbles and scattered, ruined tree trunks lying between high, steep, intimidating scree slopes, above which were forested mountains, and higher still, rocky crags that would now and then materialize out of shifting banks of cloud. This is where we'd have to climb out come dusk: up what looked like a thousand nearly vertical feet of loose gravel. I was trying not to think about it.

The river seemed smaller there, dwarfed by all that space, but in fact it was a little bigger, having taken on a few small tributaries. In places it ran for hundreds of fishless yards in shallow riffles, but true to form, every blue/green pool we came to had a few big trout in it.

While I was taking a shortcut, heading for what looked like the next bend pool on the river, I came on a small bar of washed sand with one big, crumbling, indistinct track in the middle of it and half of another right where the sand shaded into rock again. Some kind of large animal with pads and a long stride had walked through there in the not-too-distant past, but I couldn't tell what it was.

I glanced downstream. A.K. had gotten a good quarter mile ahead of me, but I could clearly see his green rain slicker against the gray expanse. I wondered if he'd fished that next pool or left it knowing I was coming along behind him. He has a gentlemanly streak in him, so it was a real possibility that he'd passed it by, but then he's also a fisherman, so maybe not.

Dave was coming up behind me, and he walked over to see what I was looking at. I pointed at the tracks and said, "I can't be sure, but I think that's a bear."

He looked, shrugged and said, "More likely a big wolf or a mountain lion." But then when he sensed my disappointment (professional guides have a nose for that sort of thing), he said, "But it's not very clear. It could be a small bear. In fact, I think it *is* a bear."

I guess he'd seen this kind of thing before: the sport who spends two days praying he won't see a grizzly bear, but who then, late on the last day, starts to get a little sorry he *didn't* see one.

Chapter 4

An Embarrassment of Riches

OVER the years I've known a number of people who have just up and quit their jobs to go fishing indefinitely. Some did it in middle age with a bankroll, others did it young and poor. Some planned it carefully in advance, others just quietly laid down their tools one day and walked, hardly even knowing what they were doing but feeling like they had wings. In some cases these folks were going through the want ads by Christmas, but in others it stuck: they became guides, or fly tiers, or sporting artists, or tackle reps, or if they couldn't find honest work, outdoor writers.

I think the urge to write comes up so often because good writing can have a lot to do with these kinds of decisions, whether they're made slowly and carefully or not. A life-changing love of fishing is learned on the water, but there are those rare stories by, say, Ernest Hemingway, Russell Chatham, Charlie Waterman and others I can't think of right now that sparkle with the kind of plain truth that can finally push you over the edge.

Robert Traver writes, "I fish because mercifully there are no telephones on trout waters." (That's less true now than when it was written, but the point is still good.) Years later a crazed angler reads that, has a moment of perfect clarity, walks up to the boss and says, "You know, there's something I've been wanting to say to you. . . . "

(I don't mean to put myself in the same category as those writers, but I have to say that once someone did tell me he'd read one of my books and it changed his life. I didn't know what to say, so I asked, "For better or worse?")

I shouldn't get overly romantic about this, because some of these have not turned out to be happy stories— the most common tragic flaw being the idea that fishing can work as revenge for a life that's gone sour. The point is, almost everyone I've known who's driven away from a job with a trunk full of fly rods has done it in the fall, usually just as the leaves began to turn.

Autumn can be the best of times and the worst of times for a trout fisher. In most of the places where trout live in North America, the best fishing starts in September and stretches through October into early November, maybe even a little later in a good year. Ten weeks, tops. The water temperatures begin to cool after a hot summer; the fish themselves are fat, healthy and hungry; the weather is comfortable to be out in and rivers, streams and lakes are all in fine shape. The days also begin to get poignantly short, and it seems like there's so much good fishing to do you can barely make a dent in it. Meanwhile the last wildflowers die, leaves turn and fall, birds fly south and all that other corny stuff, which is nonetheless corny for a reason.

It's either a glorious feast of sport or too damned much crammed into not enough time, and you can begin to see that the game may not always be here, and even if it is, you sure as hell won't.

Okay, so sporting types can get maudlin, especially those who write. A novelist I know once told me that lately he'd been confronting his own mortality. Later that summer another writer friend said, "Aw, hell, he's been saying that for twenty years." Still, there it is, staring you in the face, either at a distance or up close, and the one inscription you don't want carved on your tombstone is "The Poor Son of a Bitch Didn't Fish Enough."

I think that old urgency goes right back to the subsistence

roots of fishing, hunting and gathering. Few of us would actually starve over the winter if we didn't go out and get wild food in the fall, but then we are what we eat, and I guess I'd rather be a trout than a cabbage. Anyway, even if it's not a matter of life and death anymore, that ancestral tug you feel in the fall is still real. As my friend Ed Engle once said, "There's more biology to it than we'd like to think."

It also seems like every time I call to check out a new trout-fishing spot and ask about the best time to go, the guide says, "September and October." It's not a surprise anymore, but it's still not good news. The thing is, I have lots of fishing near home. Maybe none of it is the best you can find anywhere, but it's plenty good enough, there's a tremendous variety, and by now I know it as well as most and better than some. I love a fresh new place to go fishing as much as the next guy, but around here I can draw on twenty or thirty years of experience, so I like to stay home when home is at its best.

Of course it *is* possible to stretch things a little at each end. Here in the central Rocky Mountains, fall starts earlier at the higher altitudes, so it's possible to intercept the season at, say, 10,000 feet and follow it downhill. Or you can do the same thing by traveling north. For the last few years I've been going to fish for cutthroat trout in British Columbia, where autumn can begin in the last weeks of August. Alaska, Labrador and points in between can give you another couple of weeks.

And then some years fall lingers on for a few extra days down in northern New Mexico, while back home—remember home?—your girlfriend and your cats begin to forget you.

If you plan it just right, spend a lot of time behind the wheel and don't get screwed by the weather, you can add as much as a month to the best trout fishing of the year, but you also have to be careful. I don't know if it's actually possible to fish too much, but it *is* possible to do it too frantically, and I've noticed that I seldom fish well when I'm desperate.

Fall is also when most small-game, upland-bird and big-game hunting seasons begin, which adds another wrinkle. I do hunt, but I fish more, and that's a choice that's been forced on me over more autumns than I care to think about. (I'd actually much rather eat wild red meat and fowl than fish, even though fish is said to be brain food and I could use the help.) Anyway, hunting and fishing are both at their best, but you can't do two things at once, so you either go insane or follow your heart and see how things turn out. It turns out I'm a fisherman who hunts: a subtle but meaningful distinction.

But then there are times when you sort of *can* do two things at once, and the cast-and-blast trip is a great cure for the guy who's feeling a little conflicted. There are two I like to do around home: one is blue grouse and brook trout, the other is ptarmigan, cutthroats and maybe the odd snowshoe hare. Same mountains—sometimes even the same drainage—just different altitudes.

I usually travel a good distance on foot to get to the best spots, but it's not as cumbersome as it sounds. When I'm hunting, the three-piece fly rod stays strapped to the top flap of the day pack. When I'm fishing, I methodically unload the shotgun and stash it in a safe place before I string up the rod. And yes, there are times when I see the wrong critter for the instrument I'm carrying, but such is life.

All in all, it's a good system, but it's not foolproof. Once I wandered off fishing all afternoon, covered a lot of ground, caught lots of brook trout and then couldn't remember where I'd left the shotgun. It took me a long time to find it, and the guy I was with thought that was pretty funny. (To this day I think he knew exactly were my gun was and just wouldn't tell me, although he swears he didn't notice where I had put it.) Now I pick out an unmistakable landmark or hang a bandanna nearby.

Actually, some friends have thought the bandanna was pretty funny, too ("Memory starting to go, is it?"), but they can think what they like. A little ridicule is a fair price to pay for not losing your gun.

For a few years I had to leave the rod at home when I went deer hunting, because it was distracting. I'd spend too much time wondering how the fish were biting when I should have been thinking about hunting—that old desperation again—but after a few seasons of that I apparently got a little older and a little calmer.

Last fall I took the rod along again, and it worked just fine. The days were bright and clear and the little trout stream behind the cabin was still open, but I easily kept my mind on the deer until I had one hanging in the shed, then I put the rifle away and went fishing without a second thought. That night I even got to make this entry in my journal:

"October 13 – White River National Forest. Went deer hunting and trout fishing. Got one of each."

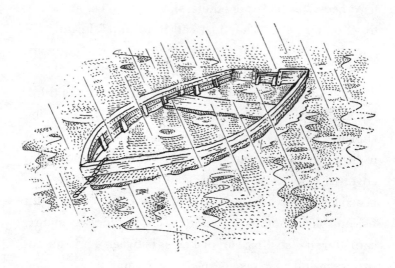

Chapter 5

Fish Camps

WHEN my friend A.K. and I got back from two weeks at a fishing camp in Labrador last year, we ran into the common western confusion about the word "camp."

"You mean you camped out?" some friends said. "Man, that's hard-core." I had to explain that in fact there was a simple square cabin with a woodstove, beds (narrow, hard beds, but beds nonetheless), a table to eat at, chairs to sit on and etc. "They just call it a camp," I said. "It's Canadian English, like adding 'ey?' to the end of every third sentence instead of 'Huh?' like we do."

But it actually goes a little deeper than that, and I think it's a useful distinction—one of those cases where the choice of language is not entirely accidental. When most of us hear the word "lodge," a lifetime's worth of exposure to advertising kicks in, and we picture vaulted ceilings, exposed log beams, a huge stone fireplace, walls covered with fish and game mounts and sporting art, leather easy chairs, carpeting, tablecloths: sort of a cross between a private trophy room and an expensive German restaurant.

Not all places that call themselves lodges are like that, but they'd all like to be and it's not all bad. When it comes right down to it, I'm not immune to the charms of a comfortable old fishing lodge, with its log walls stained by years of wood smoke and aromatic from generations of whiskey and cigars. It's just that over the long haul I tend to like things plainer than that.

When I fished with my family as a kid in Minnesota, we would drive up north to one of those ten thousand lakes and rent what the owner would usually call a "housekeeping cabin" but what my dad would more accurately describe as a "shack": four walls through which cracks of sunlight could sometimes be seen, stove, kitchen table, curling linoleum, beds with musical springs. Mosquitoes came and went at will, and there was a resident skunk or porcupine in the crawl space.

My sister would sunbathe and read, and Dad and I would fish. Ma would sometimes fish too, but wouldn't bait her own hook, and she'd cook fish—damned well—but wouldn't clean them.

For fish cleaning, there was usually an open shed with an electric light (no true fisherman would come in off the water before dark), a spigot, a pan for guts and a sawed-off baseball bat for whomping the big pike that were still alive and pissed even after the perch and bluegills had gone walleyed and stiff. The fifty-five-gallon oil drum for garbage had a lid like a bank vault and was chewed and scratched by black bears.

Catch-and-release fishing was called "throwing them back," which you only did if they were too small.

Like it or not, your values are set in childhood, so ever since then I've thought that posh surroundings were not only unnecessary on a fishing trip but possibly even inappropriate, and the few times I've been to really fancy, formal lodges I've ended up feeling at least slightly uncomfortable. Then, several years ago now, I was permanently traumatized by a week at a fishing lodge where you were expected to dress in a coat and tie for supper. The accommodations were first-class and the food was great, but the fishing was lousy, and I kept wondering, What the hell is going on here?

I'm much more comfortable at a place that calls itself a camp, if only because it probably embodies the kind of practical, blue-collar attitude that's handy for a fisherman to have. You're there to fish, and in the odd hours when you're *not* fishing, you'll need food and a dry place to sleep. With that in mind, you won't nit-pick about the ambience—or be distracted by it, either—and if you've had much experience with fish camps, you'll be pleasantly surprised to find that there's a door on the cabin.

Naturally, all camps have their own distinctive character, but there are some marked similarities, too. For instance, there's seldom the actual collection of stuffed fish you'll see at some lodges, but there's generally one: an unusually large brook trout, lake trout, char, salmon, pike or whatever. It's there as mute evidence so that even on poor days, you can tell yourself it could still happen, or in the case of faded, rotting mounts, that it at least happened once, many years ago.

There will also be a bulletin board full of photos of former clients holding big fish and either grinning idiotically or looking cold and miserable (further proof that fish are sometimes caught there), and sitting on a shelf or stuck in a windowsill, at least one huge, hideous gag fly tied on a shark hook as a joke.

Gag flies are the fly-tying equivalent of rubber vomit. Sooner or later most tiers break down and make one, realize it's nowhere near as funny as they thought it would be and never make another. Still, there the thing is, and you have to comment on it to be polite, saying something like, "The hell of it is, you could probably get a big pike on that, yuk yuk."

———

The daily drill is usually pretty basic: breakfast at camp, then out on the water with the guides, a shore lunch on a sandbar—eaten quickly while swatting bugs—supper back at camp and then out on the water again until dark, weather permitting, of course. "Weather permitting" is the unofficial motto of every fish camp I've ever been to.

Once you're actually in camp, you can either gut out bad weather or wait it out—depending on whether it's just uncomfortable or downright dangerous—but either way, at least you're there. The real drag comes when you're stuck by weather in the last outpost of civilization before you fly into camp.

There you are, reluctantly checked into a hotel near the docks where you're supposed to board the float plane, but the float planes aren't flying—and the clock on your trip is running. If you're unlucky, there will be one of those guys along who can do math in his head. He'll point out that since you've now missed a day in camp, the rest of the week's fishing will cost you $560 per day instead of $466. That's if you get in tomorrow. If you don't, the remaining days will cost . . .

At this point, someone is likely to say, "Look, shut the hell up, okay?"

The hotel itself probably isn't the Ritz or even the Holiday Inn. It's the place where fishermen, hunters, oilmen, geologists and other itinerant types stay on their way to someplace more interesting, and it's close to the docks, which is the equivalent of the wrong side of the tracks in towns that don't *have* tracks. The place is about as businesslike and sparse as the camp you're heading to: a dry bed, a lock on the door to your room and that's about it. But in daylight at least, you don't dare leave it for long because any minute someone from the camp could rush in and say, "The pilot thinks the weather's clearing. Get your stuff and let's go."

The only safe place to go before dark is down to the docks themselves, where you wander around like a lost seagull. If you're lucky you'll find something like a good-looking homemade rowboat and spend two hours standing in the rain admiring it while it slowly fills with water and begins to sink.

Sooner or later you'll wander into the small frame building that serves as terminal and international corporate headquarters of the local air service, thinking maybe there'll be some news, or at least a pot of coffee going.

This is where you run into another quirk of the Canadian conversational style, the one where, rather than answering a direct question, it's permissible instead just to sympathize with the dilemma that brought on the question in the first place. So when you ask a bush pilot, "Do you think we'll be flying into the camp anytime soon?" he'll look out the window at the gray, steady rain and say, "Yeah, she's a bugger, ey?"

All you can do is gaze out at the low, soot-colored ceiling and agree: she really *is* a bugger. These big, slow northern fronts that come in off the North Atlantic have a feeling of permanence about them, as if a new geologic age had begun. It will now rain steadily for three million years, and when it's finally over, humans will be extinct and forgotten and the dominant species in North America will be the arctic char.

When I'm marooned like that, as I have been a few times, my only real problem is a kind of social claustrophobia. After all, it's usually not just you and your fishing partner, but parties from half a dozen other camps in the area who are in the same boat. You hear the same stories over and over, look into the same fly boxes. Everywhere you go—the hotel lobby, a bar, a restaurant, even the parking lot—there are small groups of marginally despondent fishermen. They all want to talk, because there's nothing else to do, never mind that you've already discussed the weather in great detail with ten other people since breakfast.

And then every once in a while you run into one of those glad-handers from hell. The year I quit drinking, A.K. and I were stuck in a tiny north-country hotel by weather. One of the fishermen in our party decided to get drunk on some very good whiskey he'd shipped in, and for some reason it became important to him for me to get drunk, too. He was one of those good ol' boy, I'm-an-asshole-and-I'm-proud-of-it types, who wouldn't take no for an answer—although he did, finally.

It wasn't pretty, and later A.K. said, "I'm amazed you didn't hit that guy."

I said, "Don't remind me. I'll regret it for the rest of my life as it is."

It's possible to begin to unravel in situations like this,

but if you don't panic, you'll start to experience an extension of the camp mentality, which is best described as philosophical.

I guess I've been stranded like this enough times that I now half expect it, and in a strange way there have been times when I even sort of enjoyed it.

For one thing, you almost always eventually get into camp and catch some fish, and the part about getting stranded for a day or two just becomes part of the adventure, making for a better story later. I mean, it's hard to build suspense when you're telling about a trip that went smoothly from beginning to end.

And how many chances do you get to spend a day or two hanging out in a genuine outpost—a town that's either literally or figuratively at the end of the road—talking to people who actually live there, getting a glimpse into how things are done? And if life there at first seems maddeningly casual and unscheduled, doesn't that mean that you have, in fact, achieved the ultimate goal of the traveler—that is, to have finally reached a destination that isn't just like the place you left?

Of course, sometimes it's not all *that* different. My own small town in Colorado isn't at the end of any roads, but it is a fairly casual place where the pace is slow and where we usually have trouble filling up a thin weekly paper with anything you could honestly call news.

That's not to say we don't have our earthshaking stories now and then. For instance, not long ago we had a burglary. The police notes said a black bear broke into a house near here, ate all the potato chips, drank a bottle of wine and relieved himself on the kitchen floor. The bear is still at large. And then just this week news of the great pie conspiracy broke. It seems Marguerite down at the Lyons Café has lately been getting eight slices out of her homemade pies instead of the usual seven. It made the front page.

That's one of several reasons why I don't live in, say, New York City, and it's also why it doesn't drive me completely nuts to have to hang around a place like Goose Bay, Labrador, for a couple of rainy days.

On the way in on this last trip, A.K. and I were stuck in Goose Bay by weather for two extra days, along with several other parties of fishermen. Most of them were pretty patient about it, although one guy did seem to think it would help to complain about the camp owner, the hotel staff, the chicken-shit bush pilots, his travel agent and I forget who-all else. In fact, he complained for so long and left so many pregnant pauses, it became obvious he expected a reply.

Finally someone said, "Look, if the bush pilots don't want to fly, I don't want to fly either, okay?"

That was just a few minutes after someone from the camp came in and said we could forget flying in that day, because even if the weather cleared—which was doubtful anyway—there wasn't enough daylight left. You have to keep in mind that it's VFR (visual flight rules), which means no flying at night. Also, if it's an hour into the camp, it's also an hour back with the party that's waiting to come out just like you're waiting to get in, although presumably a little less anxiously. Add a few minutes for loading and unloading and a degree of slop, and you have to figure that two and a half hours before dark is when your window of opportunity slams shut.

The camp manager in Goose Bay is in communication with the camp itself by short-wave radio (when there's not too much interference), so the fishermen there probably had the same news: no flights today. That meant they had a good two hours of fishing time before dark, and I knew that at that very moment they were stringing up their rods, scrambling into rain gear and heading for the canoes. The quickest of them were probably already heading up the channel into Big Hairy Lake or down through Shear Pin Rapids toward the Caddis Flats, where if it wasn't pouring rain or blowing hard, there'd be a decent hatch and at least a few big brook trout would be rising.

I looked out the hotel lobby's small picture window at the wet, empty parking lot and had a rare, uncluttered kind thought: Good for them. I hope someone hangs a seven-pounder.

Chapter 6

Belief

PAT called me the other day with a good story. There's a little mountain lake on a ranch near here that Pat got access to a few years ago and promptly stocked with cutthroat/rainbow hybrid trout; fishermen call them cutbows. He was working there on the ranch, in a recording studio that looked like the bridge of the Starship *Enterprise* (except for the grand piano) that had been stuffed into a small log cabin, but one of the first things he did when he was setting up shop was call the hatchery. To a fisherman, a troutless body of cold water is like a car without wheels, a guitar without strings, spaghetti without meatballs.

He probably understood that the trout in the lake would distract him from the work he was there to do. Or maybe he thought a fishless lake would distract him more. He's a fly fisherman. Who knows what he was thinking?

Like most privately owned lakes, this one had a checkered past. It had been stocked haphazardly a few times over the years, but apparently never with anything that could spawn, so by the time Pat's cutbows went in, the best guess around there was that the little lake was fishless and had been for a while.

Anyway, Pat was fishing there alone one day and the dry-fly fishing was a little slow, so he tied on a weighted nymph, cast it to the deepest hole over on the south end of the lake, let it sink until he figured it was pretty much on the bottom—maybe even snarled in weeds or wedged between rocks—and then began a slow retrieve.

The fish he caught was a huge, deep-bellied rainbow no less than 24 inches long; healthy and brightly colored, but also scarred up from a long life filled with run-ins with herons and ospreys.

The biggest of the cutbows now goes maybe 17 inches, tops, and the hatchery guy swears he did not slip in a big bow, either on purpose or by accident. I've fished this lake a few times myself, but Pat, who often works within sight of it, fishes it often, knows it well and is a good, observant fisherman. In several years he'd had no clue that there was a fish of that size in there, and this is a small lake, the kind you can think you know inside out after watching it and fishing it for a few seasons. So that rainbow had to be an old fish left over from a previous stocking: once a domestic, hatchery fish, now gone as wild and spooky as a hermit.

Pat released the fish and then, after a few more casts to the same spot with the same fly, he caught it again. The same rainbow. He recognized the scars. It didn't fight nearly as hard the second time.

Things like that happen in fishing, and people always wonder why and how. I think it's because when the gods or whatever finally decide to hand you what you've been looking for, they want to make sure you don't miss the point. After all, we humans have a long history of missing the point.

Down at the core of every fisherman's heart is the belief that on any day something wonderful and unlikely could be made to happen, and that if you're careful and patient it could happen to you. It's not quite as simple as the gut certainty that there's always a bigger fish in the water than the biggest one you ever caught there (a fish can be cosmic for reasons other than size), but that probably comes close enough without getting too mystical about it.

And although catching a great fish can sometimes look like simple luck, every fisherman knows it's more than that: something like intelligent curiosity combined with cagey, skillful persistence, more like luck at poker than on a slot machine. Whatever you call it, I think a lot of us fish day after day as much for what *could* happen as for what actually *does* happen.

Quite a few years ago now, an ancient earthen dam in the Colorado Rockies near where I live burst and flooded a small trout stream, not to mention a nearby tourist town. The water from the reservoir sluiced down with enough force to make a quarter-mile-wide rocky scar on the mountainside and deposit an alluvial fan across the valley, creating a new lake (which actually fishes pretty good for brook trout). Not long after the water receded, some national park employees who were out inspecting the damage found a 30-inch-long brown trout that had been washed out of the stream. It was lying dead on a newly formed sandbar. Honest. 30 inches. That's what they said.

This was a pretty little mountain creek that people fished with dry flies and 4-weight rods. There was no place on it where you couldn't easily roll-cast to the far bank, and a 10-inch trout was considered a real nice one.

I never did see the carcass of that huge brown—it was pretty rank by the time they found it, so they measured it and then buried it—but I did talk to a biologist about it. He said this would have been a precocious, aggressive fish that had grown to 14 or 15 inches quickly on a normal diet of insects, and then started feeding on bait fish, young brook trout and maybe the odd field mouse.

The fish probably became nocturnal, spending his days in one of the deeply undercut banks in that meadow stretch, coming out at night to eat anything smaller than a muskrat that got in his way. Eventually he became a monster—in the affectionate way anglers use that term.

Chances are no fisherman ever hooked him, and if one did—casting after dark with the small fly and light line you'd use in a little creek like that—he probably thought he'd snagged a beaver by mistake and was relieved when he broke it off. This was a trout so big for the water it was in that you wouldn't have believed it *was* a trout.

No one was able to guess at exactly where this thing had lived, and it hardly mattered anyway. The trout was dead and the flood had pretty much rearranged the stream. Still, I remember this one dark, deeply undercut bend pool that looked real good but didn't seem to have the regulation pod of little browns and brookies in it.

I just shrugged it off at the time, never thinking that all the little fish had been eaten by something, and I've shrugged off other places like it since, but now there's always a nagging moment of indecision. How many pools that you don't catch a fish out of hold a brown trout as long as your leg? Damned few, actually, but . . .

Late last June Steve Peterson and I were fishing the shallow end of a warm-water reservoir. It was a hot afternoon, and the fishing was a little slow. In a couple of hours Steve had landed a small largemouth bass and a decent bluegill; I'd had a little bass and a carp.

This place is not known for its fishing, which is why we were there. Just because a body of water isn't popular with fishermen doesn't mean the fishing isn't good. It could just mean that not everyone and his brother knows about it. Over the years, some friends and I have made a practice of sniffing around spots like this. Usually not much happens, but it's paid off just often enough to keep us doing it.

Anyway, we finally lost interest in the reservoir and decided to go explore the sprawling wetland that stretched off to the west. All we could see was a mile of cattails with some scattered Russian olives, but there were some open spots we thought might be ponds.

It was pretty hard going through the tangled marsh, but there *were* some ponds, possibly odd ditches and pits left over from the construction of the dam, although they were so old and had gone so wild it was hard to tell. A whole string of them were stagnant and muddy from rooting carp, but then half a mile or so in, we came to a clear pond. It was maybe an acre or two, long and narrow with weedy shallows and a deep slot along the far bank that looked to be four or five feet deep, which is plenty deep enough for fish to winter over in this climate.

I tied on a size-10 cork popper, hoping for a bluegill, and proceeded to catch a fat, 14-inch bass that jumped three times. A few minutes later Steve got a bigger one.

As it turned out, there was a clear spring drainage running down the far end of the marsh with a string of ponds along it. Some were ankle-deep and lousy with frogs and damselflies, but apparently fishless. But then the ones with any depth and size to them had bass ranging from 9 inches to one I hooked but couldn't land that probably went two and a half or three pounds, to one I saw but couldn't catch that was bigger yet.

Approaching darkness and a nasty-looking thunderstorm drove us off before we could explore the whole thing, but we knew we had something. There were no trails in there; no cigarette butts or beer bottles or bait cans. It wasn't the kind of place that would be *completely* unknown, but few people fished the reservoir, fewer yet would take the trouble to slog back into that marsh, and it was an unlikely, easily overlooked sort of spot anyway: the kind you had to discover on your own.

Walking around the reservoir on the way back to the truck we met a woman with binoculars watching birds and a guy throwing sticks in the water for a handsome pair of labs. There were no other fishermen. The man with the dogs asked, "Do any good?" and Steve said something like "Nope, just nice to be out, though."

Ten steps farther on he said to me, quietly, "Man, days like this are why I fish."

Yeah, me too, and any day could turn out to be one of the great ones. That's why I stayed so late on that farm pond the other night. Mike Clark, Mike Price and I drove out there after supper, and as usual, we started off fishing for the sunfish: rock bass and bluegills. There are some big ones in there, and they're hard to pass up, even though we know there are also some good-sized largemouth bass.

So we caught panfish for a couple of hours, not hand over fist like you do with the little ones, but more or less steadily. It was a calm, warm evening, with an enormous white thunderhead taking up half the horizon and a third of the sky out to the east and getting bigger by the minute. It was an amazing, magnificent storm that you'd now and then stop casting to look at and that you didn't quite want to turn your back on. The cloud got brighter and brighter until, right at sunset, it turned rose-colored, flaring up from the ground wider and wider, flat on top like an anvil.

At that moment, right as the sun went off the pond and a pinkish, metallic glow spread out on the water, we caught several enormous rock bass and one huge bluegill, half again bigger than anything we'd caught since we got there. And then it shut off. Just like that: no more boils, no more strikes. I wasn't quite ready to quit yet, so I decided to tie on a size-2 Dahlberg Diver–style froggie and try for some bass.

This is a small pond—almost too small for three decent fly-casters to fish comfortably—and I know that catching a dozen big sunfish in the hour or so before dusk can stir things up pretty well, probably enough to put the bass off. The real trick here would be to show up late, alone, tie on a bass fly and sit quietly on the bank in the half dark, watching for the submarine bulge of a big fish and ignoring the boils of half-pound bluegills. But that takes a little more discipline than I'm capable of. You could end up sitting there till midnight and then just getting one cast.

I kept fishing the diver anyway because I knew—I mean, I believed—there were some big bass in there. And not just because I wanted them to be, either. The bass were there—I'd seen 12- and 13-inchers now and then. The pond was spring-fed, deep and rich with lots of cover; there were swarms of baitfish, tadpoles, bugs and crawdads; the panfish were big, which means something large and hungry was thinning out the little ones; and only three or four people had ever fished it. The big bass in there were like black holes: Nobody had ever seen one, but the universe doesn't make sense without them.

I kept casting because I only needed for one of those bass to make a mistake, and if that was going to happen, I had to have a hook in the water: the first rule of fishing. I guess I was going with belief against the odds, which is what you do when the odds tell you to give up and go home.

Finally the two Mikes were back at the truck breaking down their rods, ready to leave but too polite to say anything. (It's an unwritten law of angling that you don't mess with someone who's psyched.) By then the pond was almost black and the thunderhead had grown, marched closer while I wasn't looking and turned a dark charcoal gray and was flickering with lightning that was beginning to sound close. The gray fog of hard rain had reached a range of hills no more than a mile away, but between the rolls of thunder the air was still deathly quiet.

I knew it was about time to give it up, because I was reminding myself that it's possible to want something desperately but still be okay if you don't get it. And also that it's probably better in the long run to come back tomorrow than to get struck by lightning tonight.

There might have been a lightning strike nearby, because a bullhorn siren went off out to the southeast, probably at the Louisville Volunteer Fire Department. The siren went on for a few minutes and stopped. There was half a minute of eerie silence, and then a dozen coyotes answered it.

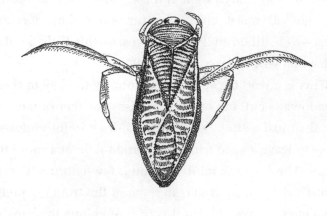

Chapter 7

Boatmen

THIS year I stumbled on something I'd read about but had never seen before in half a lifetime's worth of fly-fishing. Some friends and I were fishing a little foothills trout lake we can sometimes manage to get on. It's a spring-fed pond surrounded by rolling hay meadows set in a pretty little rimrock valley with mixed ponderosa pine and mountain mahogany petering down the west slope and scattered junipers ringing the east. Some big, fat mule deer live there, and lots of hawks, eagles and water-fowl. Most evenings, right at dusk, you'll hear coyotes. If you get all moist and romantic about the American West—as I still do after all these years—this is the kind of place that will knock you right out.

This is a working spread, so naturally the hay in those meadows is cut, but on the premise that there's more to life than just getting the horses fed, it's carefully mowed so as to leave a good fringe of riparian habitat around the shore. The lake has rainbows and a few cutthroats in it, and it's rich, buggy water, so some of the trout get pretty big. One good way to fish it is to creep along the bank in the chest-high cover and try to spot cruising trout before they spot you. And if you happen to flush the occasional grasshopper into the water ahead of you, well, that can't be helped.

This was a warm day: bright and sunny, a little breezy, temperatures in the high 70s. In the morning, there were a few trout rising sporadically to a sparse midge hatch and a few mayfly spinners left over from an earlier spinner fall—maybe from early that morning, maybe from the evening before.

For most of the morning there were some good-sized rainbows working the shallow water on the windy end of the lake, where the steady breeze had pushed a mess of spent spinners and live midges up against the bank. Some trout up to two and three pounds were cruising along there in no more than a foot of clear water under a bright

sun, eating the occasional bug as if they had nothing better to do. These were fish that would flush like quail at
the slightest movement from a fisherman on the bank, so
we had to hunker in the tall grass without so much as
blinking and pick our shots. It was a little ticklish, but we
managed to get a few.

By midday the bright sun had driven the fish into
deeper water and things really slowed down. I ended up
trolling across the lake in a float tube, killing time and
waiting for something to happen. Dragging a streamer
across a lake on a sink-tip line is not my favorite way to
fly-fish, but unless you've temporarily run out of steam,
it's better than a nap, and it's also not a bad way to hang a
real pig.

I remember that I'd lost track of the guys I was with.
Maybe they'd wandered off to one of the other lakes, or
maybe they were sleeping in the tall grass.

Anyway, I'd been across the lake a couple of times
when I saw a rise, and then another, and then two or three
more. The fish were slashing now instead of sipping as
they'd been doing to the midges and spinners that morning, and once I took the trouble to look, there were some
small but robust-looking, straw-colored bugs in the air. I
should have noticed them before, but then I was trolling,
so I was about half asleep.

I thought, Great, a caddis hatch. I switched back to a
floating line, telling myself to be calm, slow down and try
not to drop both reels in the lake. Then I tied on a #16 Hares
Ear nymph to copy the caddis emergers and started casting.

I'd throw a few feet ahead of a rise, let the fly sink for a second or two and then start a brisk but not too fast retrieve.

Caddis pupae usually swim quickly to the surface, which is why trout feeding on them make that splashy, almost angry-looking rise form, and the fish will often get on the emergers more than the winged flies. That's chapter and verse from half the how-to-catch-trout books ever written, and it's one of the first things in fly-fishing I was ever able to recognize and then make work. I guess it's pretty obvious, but if anything, it delights me more now than it did the first time. It seems like I spend most of my life wondering what the hell's going on, and this is one of the few things I can recognize and understand at a glance.

In the next hour or so, I hooked four big trout. One hit so hard he broke the fly off. (Well, okay, *I* broke the fly off. Anyway, I had to tie on a fresh one.) One ran me into my backing, jumped twice and threw the hook. I landed the other two.

While I was paddling around looking for more rising fish, I noticed some of the bugs on the surface, so I eased the float tube over to look at them. I've seen a lot of caddis hatches, but this one didn't look familiar, and the first bug I got close to didn't look right at all.

It was small—about a hook size 16 or 18—and had light tan wings with darker mottling like a standard caddis fly, but the shape was wrong. The head was too big and square, the wings were more of a dome than a peaked roof shape, there were no antennae I could make out, and there were unusually long legs sticking off each side. It looked like a capsized canoe complete with the paddles, and when I reached for it with my aquarium net, it didn't fly, it vanished straight down into the water, very quickly.

I was so convinced this was a caddis hatch it took a few seconds to register, but I realized this had to be the winged form of the aquatic water boatman beetle.

These are odd little creatures that live an even more precarious existence than most prey species. They feed on algae on the bottom, but they don't have gills, so they have to swim to the surface periodically to get an air bubble. They hold the bubble in their two pairs of short front legs and paddle back down with their long, hinged, oar-like hind legs. I don't know how many trips they make back and forth to the surface in a day, but it has to be a lot, and on each trip any hungry fish that happens to be around has a good chance at them.

And yes, they're funny-looking, as if Rube Goldberg had been put in charge of this branch of insect evolution.

I sat there in the float tube for a while watching the bugs. Some of the beetles would swim quickly to the surface and fly off immediately, and now that I knew what they were, I realized they didn't look that much like caddis flies after all. They were too round and flew with their heads too high, more like ladybugs.

Others were dropping out of the air onto the water and diving down toward the bottom. Presumably, those were the females going to deposit their fertilized eggs. Sometimes the returning bugs would hit the water so hard they'd leave a ring big enough to have been made by a rising minnow. Now and then one couldn't get through the surface tension, so it would skitter off across the top of the water until it could bore itself under. A few were sitting still on the surface, apparently resting, but most of them were swimming, plopping, skittering or flying furiously.

Bugs can be oblivious at times, but I couldn't help but think these knew that at any moment a big, dark shape could come up behind them and it would all be over. Like a lot of things in nature, this looked peaceful enough from a distance: a few bugs in the air, a few small, gently spreading rings on the water, but up close it was sustained panic.

I'd fished to water boatmen before, even had some more or less standard patterns in my nymph box: bead chain eyes for weight, dubbed body—or sometimes tinsel to copy the flash of an air bubble—shell back of mottled turkey wing or latex and something like goose biots, rubber hackle or knotted feather fibers for the legs. Some also had a strand or two of some kind of thin, crinkly tinsel trailing off the back to imitate the string of tiny bubbles these beetles sometimes leave behind them as they swim.

I even sort of know what to look for when trout are feeding on them. Usually there are a handful of fish in the shallows, and now and then you'll see a long, fast wake, followed by a furious boil, followed by stillness. You cast to the spreading rings of the boil, let your fly sink, then strip it toward the surface with very short, quick jerks.

As I said, I'd read about the mating flights, but since I'd never seen one, I'd come to think of these beetles as purely aquatic. Almost any book on still-water fly-fishing has a paragraph or two on water boatmen beetles and the very similar back swimmers. The patterns I've seen are all nymphs, usually weighted. A few books talk about mating flights, but nothing I'd seen had ever mentioned how much they resemble a caddis hatch, both in the way the bugs act and the way the trout feed on them.

To me one of the greatest kicks in fly-fishing is not only catching fish, but knowing why and feeling wise about it—at least until you realize that for the last hour or so you were dead wrong but you were catching fish anyway.

The hatch—or whatever you want to call it—was over. There were only a few bugs left and the fish had stopped rising, so I could only wonder whether I'd have caught a few more if I'd known what was going on and had the right pattern. But then you also have to wonder whether catching a few more fish is really the point.

There's nothing wrong with the entomological approach to fly-fishing—it's fun, it's interesting, watching bugs gives you something to do when the fish aren't biting, some of the patterns that come out of it are downright gorgeous, it keeps a lot of fly tiers in a job, and it even works as often as not. But there's somehow more to it than that: indefinable, intuitive stuff; fish sense, predatory alertness, something that would explain (if you *could* explain it) those guys who catch the hell out of fish without seeming to know what they're doing in any kind of refined, technical sense.

These are the guys who, after hooking four 20-inch-or-better trout and landing two of them, wouldn't be drifting aimlessly in a belly boat wondering whether or not they'd used the right fly.

I finally decided that success in nature—as opposed to success among humans—depends on nothing but day-to-day performance. Since fly-fishing sits somewhere between the two, I could always say, "Look, I caught some trout. How wrong could I have been?"

I said I'd never seen a water boatman mating flight before, but of course now I have to wonder about that, too. Fact is, I probably *have* seen it and just didn't know what I was looking at. After all, I'd just fished this thing as a caddis hatch and caught some nice big trout, which is the kind of thing an angler who thinks of himself as a fair-to-middling amateur naturalist offers as absolute proof.

So I guess the moral is, proof isn't always proof after all. Or maybe it's that even honest fishing stories can't always be trusted. But I guess you knew that already.

I drifted out there for a few more minutes watching a ranch hand mow hay across the valley. The day was almost hot, but the breeze was sweet-smelling and cool. At four hundred yards or so the growl of the tractor was pleasantly quiet and the driver was perched comfortably on the seat with one hand held lightly on the wheel, taking in the scenery, with his hat cocked back at the precise angle that Will Rogers used to wear his. It's sights like that that sometimes make me pine for the days when I did real work.

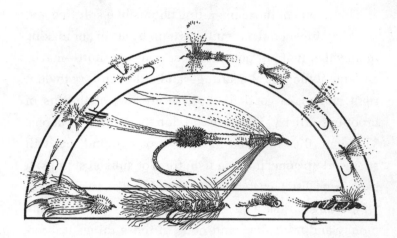

Chapter 8

Patterns

I'VE been tying flies lately, filling a few empty slots with old standards I've burned up so far this season and putting together a few new specialty patterns they swear I'll need for some trips that are coming up. Of course I already have boxes full of flies I tied for other trips and then didn't need after all, but if I hadn't tied them I probably *would* have needed them, and somehow it seems better this way.

This is one of those unending chores like splitting and stacking firewood that you'll burn up by spring or making money that will just get spent. Sessions are short—maybe an hour at the vise at a sitting—and although I try to do it right and make good flies, there are few of the fits of brooding artistry I'll have on long winter afternoons. These are flies I'll need in a week or two and that will soon end up gone: hung in fish, trees or sunken stumps. It can seem a little existential at times, but it's satisfying. After all, three things a guy needs to live are warmth, a little money and trout flies, and none of those things last forever.

Tying a batch of flies always takes me a while, because I'm one of those slow, meticulous tiers who'll half untie the thing or even start all over again if something isn't quite right. I don't think fly tying is an art, but any good fly *is* beautiful in its own way, and it can get the kind of gut response from a trout that any artist would die for.

There's a kind of romance about tying some patterns that I really enjoy. Things are a little more homogenized now than they used to be—that's inevitable when a once cranky little sport becomes a big business—but there are still strong regional tendencies to fly patterns. For instance, a dusky-colored, divided-wing Green Drake dry fly says Frying Pan River in Colorado, while the same fly tied greener with slate-colored, almost black wings says Henry's Fork in Idaho—to me anyway, as well as to a few poor, dumb fish.

It's probably the same big mayfly on both rivers—or at

least close to it—so logically the same pattern should work well in both places, but then the point where logic breaks down is where life and fly-fishing both really start to get interesting.

Tying for new water involves a different kind of romance. The guy says the Woolly Buggers *must* have a body of pale dirty green with a dyed olive grizzly hackle and a short tail of mottled marabou-like fluff from the base of an olive grizzly saddle feather. I can't believe my old olive-and-black ones wouldn't work, but I tie the new flies anyway, they're real pretty, and I wonder, What is it about this fly that speaks the unique language of that river?

And then there are the truly weird patterns, without which this sport would be as dull as golf. A fly-fisher I know in England once sent me a fly called a Toenail Shrimp. It has a body of rough, blond seal fur, a wire rib and a shell back made from a human toenail clipping. This is one that'll never catch on big because, if nothing else, you'd have a hell of a time getting enough material to tie them commercially. On the bright side, the stuff does come in a nice range of sizes.

By the way, I'm passing this along on faith. The guy swears it's a real pattern that real fishermen in Ireland use, but if it's not, it won't be the first time I was had by straight-faced British humor.

It's interesting what's happened with fly patterns over the last, say, twenty years. I almost said there were fewer of them back then than there are now, and that's probably true enough, although way back in 1950, when J. Edson Leonard published his book *Flies,* there was a section in the back listing some 2,200 fly patterns. True, he had to reach nearly all the way back to the dawn of the sport to assemble that many, but they were, nonetheless, bona fide patterns.

I guess that's my point. The idea of an actual fly *pattern,* calling for specific materials to be tied onto a hook in a specific way and then to be called by a specific name, has begun to get pretty fuzzy around the edges. Where once you could ask someone if they tied Blue-Winged Olive dry flies and expect a straight answer, you now have to ask, "*How* do you tie your Blue-Winged Olives? As a parachute? Okay, what do you use for a wing post?"

Plenty of fishermen still use the original Don Gapen Muddler Minnow—I just caught a big rainbow on one the other day—but since it was first tied back in the 1930s, it has spawned an extended family of fatheaded Muddler/Spuddler/Sculpin/bullhead sorts of things, including the inevitable Frankenstein patterns like the Bow River Bugger, a great streamer that was born, the story goes, when a mad scientist in Alberta grafted the head of a Muddler onto the body of a Woolly Bugger.

That sort of thing goes on all the time, and it makes a kind of theoretical sense. If the Muddler and the Bugger are both good patterns, then a hybrid could be even better. Sure, it could be worse, too, but you'll never know unless you try it.

The thing is, there are a lot more fly tiers than there used to be, supported by a lot more books, videos, classes and live demonstrations and a whole new raft of plastic tying materials, and fly patterns themselves have become a form of self-expression. That's neither good nor bad, although I *am* glad I learned to tie back when actual patterns were regarded with more reverence. I had even more trouble with discipline then than I do now, and I think it was good for me to have a recipe to follow and a model to copy. It kept me from wandering off on my own too much, at least at first.

It's like an old college art professor of mine used to say: "Freedom must be exercised with—not instead of—restraint." We made fun of him at the time because he was over thirty and a little pompous, but we knew he was right.

Of course, fly patterns have always evolved. When Leonard Halladay first tied the Adams dry fly back in the 1920s, it was a down-wing pattern. By the time I learned to tie it, it had become an up-winged fly, and that was how one tied it "correctly." In the early seventies, I found it in Jack Dennis's first book, *Western Trout Fly Tying Manual,* with a tail of moose hair instead of the original hackle fibers because that made it float better. I use that pattern now—sometimes known as a Western Adams— which incorporates two changes from the original over a period of no less than five decades. By modern standards, that's really conservative.

But that's not to say I have anything against the

Delaware Adams or the Parachute Adams or any of the other Adamses out there. I don't even regret coming up with a ginger-colored Adams myself once in a rainy-day, caffeine-induced fit of creativity.

I actually caught fish on that fly, and over the years, I've caught fish—and seen them caught—on some pretty ridiculous patterns. In fact, it's occurred to me it would be an interesting exercise to try and tie a fly that *wouldn't* catch a fish sooner or later, but then when I look through the books, magazines and catalogues, it becomes obvious that plenty of people are at work on that already.

I once got into a philosophical discussion with some people at a company that wholesales flies about just what constituted a new fly pattern—that is, one that's new enough that the so-called originator could legitimately put his or her name on it. Does a new fly have to be completely unique, using materials, techniques and designs that have never been seen before? Probably not. Then again, does changing the wing color and the name of an existing pattern make it a new fly or just a monument to a tier who's taking himself too seriously?

At this stage of the game, I think it's almost impossible to come up with something genuinely new, even if that's all you're trying to do. (Across campus from my old art professor's office was a philosophy teacher who liked to say, "There have been no new ideas since Plato.") I've fooled around with fly patterns a lot over the years, but I've never come up with anything that was better than—or even very different from—the standard stuff, and once I independently invented a fly that turned out to be over four hundred years old. Now and then I've tweaked other people's patterns just enough to make them feel like my own, the same way I've adapted some recipes in cooking, but I can't claim to have invented the hamburger.

I did once put my name on some patterns that were nothing but variations on existing flies—and of course I did it in print so I couldn't take it back later—but I never felt quite right about it. In one of his great food stories, Jim Harrison says, "Attribution is important in cooking," and it should be in fly tying, too, in the interest of accuracy and so you don't end up looking like a thief.

I don't know what the wholesale fly company finally decided about originality, but *I* decided that fly patterns are like literature: endless variations on a handful of themes. The good ones are the ones that work, for whatever reason, and the great ones are those that survive beyond their own generation.

Speaking of which, I was just flipping through Mary Orvis Marbury's great old book *Favorite Flies and Their Histories*. This thing was published in 1892, fifty-eight years before Leonard published *Flies,* with its 2,200 patterns, and it listed a mere 291 flies. Some of them seemed vaguely familiar to me—probably from other illustrations in other old books—but there were only a handful that I'd ever seen in the flesh and none that I'd actually fished. And I think of myself as a traditionalist.

But even back then this business of fly tying was pretty much as it is now. According to Ms. Marbury, "Whenever a bilious angler has no luck, and nothing to do, he sits down and concocts a new swindle in feathers . . . and at once every angler in the country rushes in and pays two dollars a dozen for samples."

Actually, there is one familiar fly in that old book: the Royal Coachman wet fly, tied with a tail of black and white barred wood duck flank and wings of white duck quill. It's familiar because back in the 1930s the great Lee Wulff began tying the dry-fly version of it with hair wings and tail and renamed it the Royal Wulff. You can buy one today in any fly shop in America.

According to Marbury, the Royal Coachman was first tied in New York City in 1878 by John Haily as a variation of the plain old Coachman wet fly that probably came over on the *Mayflower*.

I have a lot of flies—maybe too many—because I fish a lot and I've tied for a long time now. But when I'm getting ready for a trip, the first thing I want to know is, What flies do I need? Now and then it's something I already have, though usually it's something new and strange, like size-4 Hexagenia limbata wiggle emergers with gills and eyeballs. Whatever they are, I tie them dutifully (following directions, or better yet, copying a sample), all the time thinking, What the hell, if the fishing wasn't different from what it is at home, why go?

I want a sample because fly patterns are like recipes: They come out differently depending on the cook, and sometimes little elements of style make all the difference.

Even when I've already tied flies for a trip, I usually carry an empty fly box for the flies I'll probably buy when I finally get there. I'm a sucker for patterns I've never seen before on sale at a fly shop right on the bank of the river, especially if the bin they're in is already half empty. I always think, Who knows more than the local fishermen?

But at the same time, I'm not entirely convinced that there's such a thing as The One Right Fly, even though I seem to spend half my time on the water searching for just that. One of my favorite things about fly-fishing (because it keeps it from becoming an exact science) is that fly patterns work differently for different fishermen.

I was floating a river in Canada not long ago and our guide was pushing a thing called a Turk's Tarantula, a big, nondescript, rubber-legged dry fly that he said the fish went wild for. A.K. and I were whacking them just fine on size-10 and -12 hoppers, but the guide kept waving this Tarantula at me, so I finally tied it on. In the next mile A.K. caught over a dozen good fish and I didn't get a strike. Finally I foul-hooked a 6-inch trout and said to the guide, "There, you happy?"

He said, "It worked for the last guy."

Maybe there's actual magic in that, or maybe you just fish the same pattern with a more deft and realistic action than I do. Or maybe any angler fishes a fly he really likes better than one that leaves him sort of cold.

Whatever it is, I've been on lots of trips where the guy on my left is getting them on a black Flash-a-bugger, the guy on my right is whacking them on a #10 green damsel nymph, and I'm doing well enough on a #16 Hares Ear. And even if I did want to change, *my* green damsel probably isn't the same as *his* green damsel.

The real truth is, convincing a fish to strike is like playing string with a cat: the exact size and color of the string is probably less important than how you wiggle it.

And little cats are easier to fool than big ones.

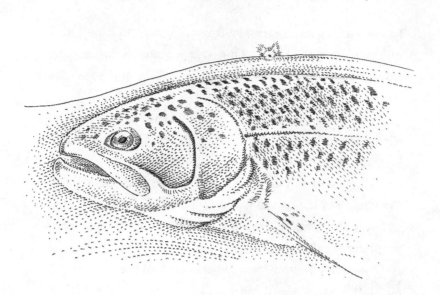

Chapter 9

Getting Stuck

I DON'T know how it is that you get stuck on one seemingly uncatchable trout when there are hundreds of easier ones in the same river. Maybe it's because he's big (the hard ones often *are* big), or maybe it's the challenge, or curiosity, or something so inexplicable it just boils down to the nature of your own particular demon.

Once a friend of mine spent all afternoon—a good four

hours—trying for a nice-sized brown trout that he never did catch. Later I said, "That was a smart fish," and he said, "Yeah, I was gonna kill 'im and eat 'im just to get the son of a bitch out of the gene pool."

The last time it happened to me was on the Frying Pan River in western Colorado. A.K., Mike Clark and I had been fishing there for three days with no set date for breaking camp and heading home. As on previous trips to the Pan, the plan was to fish either until we'd had enough or until someone felt the need to go back and get some work done.

Of course we know from experience that these trips usually last about a week, but not having an actual schedule gives them an open-ended feeling we all like. We've been making this trip—usually with Ed Engle—for . . . Well, I guess that's when something becomes a tradition: when you can't remember how long you've been doing it.

It was mid-September, which is always sort of a poignant milestone in Colorado fly-fishing: It's not the last of the dry-fly fishing by a long shot, but it's usually the last of the best. We'd had mixed hatches of mayflies: Green Drakes, two sizes of Blue-Winged Olives, Pale Morning Duns, Sulphurs and the odd Red Quill, plus some midges and small crane flies to further confuse things. On the water, the little yellow crane flies on the Pan can look a lot like Pale Morning Duns. Fishermen often can't tell the difference, but the trout can.

The weather was clear and crisp—seasonable for a high mountain valley on the west slope of the Rockies. Later in the year it can get pretty grim in that country, but in September the chill feels friendly and invigorating. Still, the second camp chore each morning—after starting coffee on the propane stove—was to get a fire going for warmth.

I'd found the fish on the afternoon of the previous day when I worked my way up to a long, pretty bend pool that had a nice pod of trout rising to Blue-Winged Olives. I got two or three fish on a #20 Olive parachute, and then spotted a big one up near the head of the pool. He was in a broken, choppy slick between two faster currents, rising in that casual, unhurried way the big trout have: no splashing, no darting, all business. I'd see a big head materialize for a split second, and if he turned just right in the light, the quick flash of reddish orange, olive and silver that meant he was a rainbow.

I got in what I thought was the best position for a good cast and fished for him methodically as the hatch shaded from one bug to another to another—changing flies and hooking two other trout by accident in the process—until I thought I'd put him down. Then I realized he'd quit rising because it was getting on toward dusk and the hatch was over. My shoulders were sore from being locked in the unconscious, predatory hunch; my legs were half numb from standing in cold water, and it occurred to me a cup of coffee around the campfire would feel pretty good.

Neither of my friends had ever gotten closer than fifty yards to me that afternoon, but there must have been something about my body language, because on the drive back to camp A.K. said, "You had a pig going in there, didn't you?"

"Yup," I said.

"Did you get him?"

"Nope. By the way, how long was I up there?"

"I don't know," A.K. said, "all afternoon."

At that time of year on the Frying Pan, the hatches don't usually start until mid-morning at the earliest, so we often spend an extra half hour in camp drinking boiled coffee with eggshells and discussing where to fish. But the next morning I was out early, saying I knew where I was going. Mike and A.K. smiled wisely and said they knew I knew and they knew where, as well. Meaning, I think, You found him, let him drive *you* nuts.

The spot actually held two pools, the big, long one I'd been fishing and a smaller one upstream. Above that the water was posted, and below it, just out of sight, was a long run right along the road: an obvious place that was good nymph-fishing water and often had fishermen in it, sometimes with guides. I can't say my spot was an unknown little corner, because the Pan is a famous, mostly public river that doesn't *have* any unknown corners, but I do think it's not fished as much as some of the other stretches.

I got there early anyway—to beat any possible competition—and stood around for what seemed like a long time before I saw a rise near the tail of the pool. Then I looked on the water and saw the first Blue-Winged Olives. That fish, about a 10-inch brown, ate a #20 quill-bodied Olive parachute dry fly on the second or third drift. By then a few more trout had started rising and I missed one, then hooked another that got off after a few seconds.

I'd been watching the spot at the head of the pool, and sure enough, once the hatch got going, The Fish started to rise. I got in my old position—across and slightly upstream—and started casting with what three other trout had thought was the right fly. It took me quite a few casts to get a good drift in the complicated swirls and eddies, and when I did get my fly over the rainbow he just looked at it. I mean he turned toward it, tipped upward in the current, then thought better of it and casually ate the next natural fly that came along.

There are two schools of thought on the refusal rise. One says that if the fish was interested enough in your fly to turn and look at it once, you should keep putting it over him until his resolve weakens. (This would be like voting for Republicans all your life, thinking that sooner or later you're bound to get a good one.) The other school, the one I subscribe to, says that if he didn't like it enough to bite it the first time, what's going to change? I mean, it's still the same fly, right?

So I switched from the parachute to a collar-hackled number with divided, hackle-tip wings. Same fly, same size, different style. (Those of us who believe the refusal rise is definitive carry lots and lots of flies.)

An unknown number of casts later, I'd about decided

the fish wasn't even going to glance at my fly and I was considering changing to yet another version of the Blue-Winged Olive, when I noticed some Pale Morning Duns on the water, mixed in with the olives. If I see Pale Morning Duns on the water by themselves, I usually have to wade out and catch one in a dip net to be sure what it is, but when they're mixed with the Olives I can see from some distance that they're a size or two larger and yellower with sparklier wings. And when the light's good I can also tell they're not those crane flies, having made that mistake often enough in the past.

So I dug out a Pale Morning Dun pattern that A.K. ties. Without going into detail, this fly differs in several well-considered ways from what most fishermen think of as a PMD, and because of that, it works beautifully, and I buy them and fish them without reservation.

I have two hard-and-fast rules on flies: (1) I tie my own, period, (2) except for those patterns that someone else ties better.

Everyone has some kind of program when it comes to flies. A.K., a professional tier, really does fish almost exclusively with his own patterns, while Mike, being a bamboo rod maker, once said, "Flies should be tied by fly tiers. Just tell me what's working and I'll buy a dozen."

The fish looked at the Pale Morning Dun. In fact, he looked at it so closely that his big head bulged the water under the fly and it bobbled in the current, but he didn't actually take it and I didn't strike, although it took nerves of steel not to.

I carefully waded out of the pool, walked down the

bank to the tail and cast the fly to some of the fish rising down there. I caught two and missed a third. Nothing wrong with the pattern.

There were at least a dozen trout rising in the bottom end of that pool, some of which, I knew, would eat the flies they were supposed to eat, which meant I could catch them. But then the big head came up again, so I waded back up there, opened my small dry-fly box and began studying the six or eight different patterns I carry that could work for a Pale Morning Dun, hoping to be struck by inspiration.

It was easy enough to find my old spot, because by then I'd worn a small depression in the gravel.

This business of changing fly patterns, looking for the right one, is central to the sport. All of us, secretly or otherwise, believe it's the fly that makes the difference, although we'll admit that even the right fly has to be cast accurately and drifted properly to work. Still, when someone is catching more fish than we are—and when we're not too embarrassed to ask—we say, "What fly are you using?" as if that one bit of information was all we needed.

Okay, but if you ask three different fishermen you'll probably get three different answers, so you have to sus-pect that although the knowledge passed on by other fly-fishers is a great gift, the true solution is somehow yours and yours alone.

Everyone I know who has fly-fished for long has theories about fly patterns, all of which sound reasonable enough on a long drive or around a campfire. If Mike is along, he'll listen patiently and then ask, "But does it work?" It's surprising how often that's followed by an uncertain pause.

A.K. believes, among other things, in exactly matching the color of the real bugs. He believes in it so deeply that he dyes his own fly-tying materials to exact formulas in foul-smelling, bubbling vats in his basement and has written a good book on dying and bleaching fur and feathers.

I match colors approximately at best and rely more on shape, texture and lots of variations in pattern so I can change flies for hours without having to give up.

When A.K. and I get to agonizing over fine points of hackling, winging and coloration, Mike will just shrug at us, the same way we shrug at him when he goes on about the difference a thousandth of an inch can make eight inches up the midsection of a 5-weight bamboo fly rod.

We all catch fish, and in private moments we all think that in the long run, we catch a few more than the other two.

I don't know how many hours I spent at that pool. I was there at lunchtime and ate my ham sandwich sitting on the bank. (Mike had been in charge of the food for this trip. He'd spent most of the budget on one twenty-pound ham and half a dozen loaves of bread.) The big fish stopped rising for a while—one sloppy cast too many, I think—and I went up to the small plunge pool above and caught two small trout, a brown and a rainbow. When I came back, he was feeding again.

At one point the hatch changed from Olives to Green Drakes to PMDs and Sulphurs so quickly that I made three fly changes in a row without making a single cast. Finally I had to stop, take a few deep breaths and calm down. The more time I spend on a single fish, the more tightly wound I get. I know it doesn't help.

And then I just caught the fish. He ate a #18 Blue-Winged Olive emerger with such matter-of-fact confidence that I was almost too surprised to set the hook. He fought well, too, running me up and down the pool, taking line from the reel, jumping twice. I tried to be cool and careful, but I think if he'd broken off or thrown the hook I'd have cried and spat and pulled out hair.

He was lovely: deep-bellied, humpbacked, with a slightly kyped jaw full of small, sharp teeth. I don't carry a scale or tape measure, so I had to guess at his size. I seem to recall trying to do that honestly and coming up with no less than 19 inches, knowing that a fat fish looks longer to me than a thin one and that my first guess (21) probably included 2 inches of relief and adrenaline.

When I released him he shot strongly out into the current and dissolved into the rubble-rock bottom. I saw right where he went and right where he stopped, but I couldn't see him anymore. I believe in releasing most fish, and this was a catch-and-release area anyway, but I have to say some are harder to let go of than others.

Then I sat on the bank for a while wondering what had just happened. That is, wondering if I'd finally done it right or if he'd finally done it wrong.

It had been the first time I'd tried that little soft hackled emerger, so maybe it really was the fly pattern that made the difference. Maybe if I'd tried that fly first instead of last, I'd have caught him on the second cast the day before.

Then again, the weather had changed. For the first time in two days a squall had blown in from the Continental Divide; the sky had turned gray and a little breeze and drizzle had ruffled the water. In fact, I was wearing my rain slicker, even though I didn't exactly remember putting it on.

Most fly-fishers believe that trout bite better under gray skies than clear ones, and if that's what made the difference, maybe any fly I had on at the moment would have done it.

I've sat on other banks pondering the same things before and I've always ended up reaching the same conclusion: The question is probably more fun than the answer would be.

There were still some trout rising in the pool, but I decided I needed a break and a walk. Right then I didn't really care if I caught another fish that day or not, although I knew I'd get over that soon enough.

I waded downstream around the bend and ran into A.K., who was working his way slowly upstream. He looked up from casting and said, "Did you get him?"

"Yup."

"How big?"

"Oh, maybe nineteen inches," I said, trying to sound confident, but also modest, leaving open the possibility that it had actually been 20 inches or longer.

A.K. said, "All right," and I could tell from his expression he was automatically subtracting two inches. I remember thinking, I should have said, "Twenty-one, easy," but of course it was too late.

Then A.K. waded upstream to the pool and started casting to the fish that were still rising there. It wasn't until then that I realized I'd been selfishly hogging the same good spot for the better part of two days and neither of my friends had said a word about it. But I guess that's why they're friends: they know that when their turn comes, I'll return the favor.

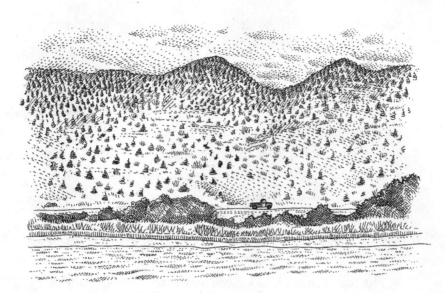

Chapter 10

Getting Skunked

GETTING skunked is something every fisherman must learn to do with some grace because it does happen. You go fishing and catch nothing, and no euphemism like "Well, it was pretty damned slow" can change that. Now and then events even conspire against the experts—and damned few of us are experts.

There are actually some codes of conduct covering

this, but they all come down to not trying to lay blame where it doesn't belong. When you don't catch fish it's pretty rare for it to be the fault of your tackle or your fishing partner, and the weather is just the weather—nothing personal. Same goes for the river and the fish themselves, which, after all, don't owe you anything.

There *are* some poor fishing guides, but as long as he gets you to the water (and as long as you know how to fish), I doubt even the devil himself could keep you from catching a fish or two when the fishing is good. When the fishing is bad, the best guide in the world can't do much about it.

The fact is, most blank days are the ones when, for one reason or another, you probably shouldn't have gone fishing in the first place if all you wanted to do was catch something. A case in point:

Last year Pat Leonard, Mike Clark and I made what we later realized was an amateur-level error in timing: We went down to fish one of our favorite stretches of the South Platte River on Martin Luther King Day. It was the third day of a classic Colorado January thaw—bright, sunny, highs in the 60s—the kind of weather that can really wake up a tailwater trout stream, maybe even bring on a little midge hatch.

But it was also a federal holiday, so the crowds were horrendous. There were carloads of fishermen driving up and down the county road along the river, small herds of fishermen wandering the banks looking despondent and at least one or two fishermen casting to every spot that might have held a trout, as well as to plenty of spots that surely didn't hold one.

There were so many fishermen wading around in the water that in places the river was choked with dislodged aquatic vegetation, the kind of thing that fouls your nymphs and makes you brood about the ecological impact of too many fishermen on too few trout streams.

Yes, we knew the South Platte was a famous and popular river no more than an hour's drive from Denver, and we knew what good weather on a midwinter holiday means on water like that. We just got excited about the warm temperatures and forgot what day it was until we came around the last bend in the canyon road and saw all the cars and people. One of us said, "Shit, that's right, it's a holiday."

Now, if it had been another time of year—say, September—we could have turned around and driven to some other, less famous and less crowded stream in the area, but in January in the Rocky Mountains you don't have a lot of choices: It's either a tailwater that stays open through the winter or it's ice fishing. So we joined all the other fishermen, each one of whom probably drove around that same bend, had the same initial thought and came to the same conclusion: Fish here or don't fish at all.

I won't bore you with a detailed description of the fishing except to say we cast to the few momentarily vacant stretches of water we could find, and by the end of the day Pat thought he might have had a halfhearted strike, but he couldn't actually swear to it. It could just as well have been a gob of weeds bumping the leader.

Still, we dutifully went through the motions, even to changing flies now and then. And if our hearts weren't completely in it, we were at least in that four-dimensional universe we all know and love: the one where there's width, height, length and current speed.

I also have to say that even though there were way too many fishermen for the water and everyone could see that, there was no animosity to speak of, just some resignation. Some fishermen cast grimly and silently; others waved ironically; some seemed oblivious, as if they'd meditated themselves into a place where the crowd didn't exist; a few shrugged and grinned sheepishly as if to say, I guess if one of us had been smart enough to stay home, the other would have a little more elbow room.

No one seemed to be doing any better than we were, and that was comforting (It could have been far worse; we could have been the only ones not catching fish), and the only trout I saw on had been foul-hooked. The guy who did that was just upstream from me and he proudly told me what fly pattern he was using.

I almost said, "If you're butt-hooking them, it doesn't *matter* what pattern you're using," but then I remembered the nature of the holiday and who'd be off work. I thought if I got him riled he might go postal on me, so I kept quiet.

Sometime in midafternoon we stopped at the little general store at Deckers to see if they had a pot of coffee on. They didn't. The woman behind the counter asked how the fishing was.

Mike said, "It's pretty poor."

She said, "That's funny, it was great yesterday."

Out in the parking lot, Pat said he was beginning to think that people behind the counters of general stores near rivers were actually robots programmed to say "You shoulda been here yesterday" whenever the subject of fishing came up.

It sounded like an unkind wisecrack, but I think it was directed not at the nice lady in the store but at the general nature of reality. In other words, I have no doubt that we really *shoulda* been there yesterday, and it stung all the worse to hear that, knowing it was true.

"Programmed by who?" I wondered.

We ran through the usual conspiracy-theory suspects (aliens, the CIA, the phone company, Newt Gingrich) and decided it could be just about anyone except the tackle industry.

We finally located some coffee at an all-but-deserted little bar a few miles up the road and spent some time formulating an elaborate theory about why we weren't catching fish. I don't remember it all now, but it seems like it had something to do with barometric pressure, sunlight, aquatic insect drift migration patterns, sunspots, continental drift, and maybe a few too many fishermen. It hardly matters. The point is, a true angler must have a detailed, scientific-sounding theory about why he's getting skunked. Only a beginner would admit that it's because the fish just ain't bitin'.

A TV was on in the corner of the ceiling, turned a little too loud to ignore. It was an old biker movie with a young

Jack Nicholson playing a reluctant Hell's Angel. I thought I'd seen it before. If I remembered right, it was unmemorable.

Taped to the wall over the bar were, I'll guess, two hundred one-dollar bills on which customers had written things they thought were amusing, apparently an old house tradition. I read the nearest thirty or so. None of them were remotely funny. One said, "Tom & Mike, Radical Trout Bums." I read it aloud. Pat said, "No real trout bum would piss away a whole dollar like that."

Then we drove along the river for a while, counting fishermen, and finally spotted a good run we knew of that was empty at the moment. Mike said, "You guys get out and grab it. I'll go park the truck and meet you in a few minutes." (We all hate to fish in a crowd, but we do know some of the tricks.)

Pat and I had been casting to the run for about ten minutes when Mike walked up and said, "See that guy I parked next to? He said he just fished this for two hours and fifteen minutes without a strike."

Pat said, "Gee, that's encouraging."

It was getting to be evening, with its gray shadows and chilly air. The strip of sky above the canyon rim had turned from kingfisher blue to pale slate, not quite dark enough for stars. It was maybe four-thirty, quarter to five, and with no clouds to hold in the weak warmth of the day it was going to be a brutally cold night. This wasn't the shortest day of the year, but it wasn't long past it either: still the dead of winter.

There was quite a bit of traffic going up the canyon as one fisherman after another gave up and headed home. Faces peered at us from some of the cars with those blank but expectant expressions fishermen come to recognize. They were thinking, Those guys are still on the water. Does that mean they're catching fish? Maybe they're waiting for dark. Should *we* be waiting for dark instead of going home?

I know what they were thinking because I've thought it myself at the end of many a slow day. If there's so much as one fisherman left on the river when you leave, you feel like a coward and a fool. You suddenly see that one more fly change and ten more casts would have done it. There's still a trout in there with your name on it, and now that guy's gonna get it.

But all we were doing was standing there telling stories about fishing trips that had been even worse than this one: trips where there were no fish for days on end, or where not catching fish was the least of it compared with more awful disasters that piled themselves on one after another like the Great Wheel of Karma itself. Every fisherman who's been at it a while has a few of these tucked away (the best proof that things could be worse is that they *have* been worse), and they're actually fond memories in a left-handed sort of way. They show that most calamities turn comic given enough time and that sometimes the best thing about the past is just that you lived through it.

Stories like that are usually no more or less true than

other fishing stories. What I mean is, fishermen probably *are* liars, but if we make the good stuff better than it really was, we also make the bad stuff worse, and we believe that in the long run that balances out to be something very much like the truth.

We're still fishing after all these years with no end in sight, and that's something, too. After all, fishing is a test of character, but it's a test you can take over as many times as you want.

Finally someone said, "Well, at least we're not thirty miles from camp in the Northwest Territories with a storm coming, night falling, a broken outboard and the guide passed out drunk."

That seemed to settle it. We walked back to the car and drove to the restaurant where we always stop for supper on the way home from the Platte. It was closed.

Chapter 11

Ponds

WHEN I was a kid, guessing from the way the two words were used by the men I fished with, I thought the difference between a pond and a lake was size: a pond was little and a lake was big.

Actually, a lake often *is* big, but its main characteristic is that it's natural, while a pond, according to the *Oxford English Dictionary,* is "A small body of still water of artificial formation." In Middle English it was "ponde" or "pounde," meaning an enclosure of some kind, like a corral or a pen. It's the same old word that gave us pound, as in a place to collect and store stray animals, and impoundment, where the same thing is done with water.

Okay, so I grew up and learned how to use a dictionary (my fourth-grade teacher, who threatened to beat me with one, would be proud), but I guess my childhood definition still stands. It's a pond if I can fish most of it—or at least enough of it—from shore; if my fishing partner can yell, "Try the olive midge" from the other side of it and I can understand him; if, as Bob White recently said, you can fish all the way around it easily in a single session.

You might feel the need for a belly boat on a pond, but if the thing cries out for a canoe, it's either a lake or a reservoir.

A pond can also be kept under wraps in a way that a stream or river or lake never can be. It can be so neatly hidden behind a hill or a line of trees that you'll never know it's there unless you walk over and look or someone takes you there. Most ponds are private, and that's just the nature of the beast (another working definition of pond could be "a small reservoir for personal use"), but because of that they can be exceptional fisheries for their size.

Peter Høeg once wrote, "The plans you keep secret are the ones most likely to succeed." The same goes for places to fish.

I've always loved to fish ponds, if only because most of them strike me as being about the right size. Ponds are large enough to have some secrets and eccentricities, but not so vast and inscrutable that you can't eventually figure them out, and the ones I never did figure out just seem like the exceptions that prove the rule.

Actually, I think most ponds are a little harder to fish than most streams. In flowing water, trout know to let the current do most of the work, so you can just look at the water and make a fair guess at where they'll be. In still water, trout have to move around looking for food, so they could be anywhere. You have to be cautious and patient, but somehow you feel you have the time for that. A good pond is a small disk of still water off by itself; self-contained, restful, permanent. Unlike a river, a pond isn't going anywhere.

And it's a modest kind of operation. It's not too much of a pipe dream to think that maybe someday you could have a little pond of your own.

On most ponds I not only try to resist the urge to get out there in a craft of some kind, I sometimes even leave the hip boots in the truck to keep myself from wading. I feel more mobile on my feet, I cast better, and since I'm much higher than when I'm in a float tube or a canoe or up to my waist in water, I'm at a better angle to spot trout.

Another reason to stay out of the water is that pond edges can hold a lot of fish. That's especially true in the mornings, in the evenings and at night, but I've fished ponds where trout cruise the grassy banks for beetles and hoppers even in the middle of hot summer days. I've often done well on ponds by hunkering down and casting up along the shore as if it were the near bank of a stream.

Of course not all ponds are great fisheries. You don't just need water, you need water of the right chemistry and temperature and turbidity and depth and volume of flow, not to mention aeration, vegetation, structure, food base and the right kind of trout, bass or panfish.

I also think you need *some* size to the thing. I don't know how small a reservoir has to be before it's a pond, but at less than an acre, a pond begins to flirt with being a puddle.

A few of the best ponds I've seen had just been left alone, but most were managed for more or less wild populations of fish. Pond management is an art. I don't know much about the particulars of that, but I do think I can recognize the results.

Over the years, on long drives home or sitting in cafés, some interesting philosophical questions have come up about ponds. Can a pond fishery be "natural" in the finest sense if the pond itself, by definition, is artificial? Probably not. If you're that much of a perfectionist, the best you can hope for from most ponds is the calculated appearance of a natural fishery.

But then another good question is, What's the difference? or maybe, How wise is it to look behind the scenes of something that's apparently beautiful? If you become too much of a purist, damned little will ever be good enough for you. You'll begin to wonder how much of the rest of your life is also an illusion and sink into a full-blown existential crisis. Eventually you'll end up living a disappointing life and your nonfishing friends (if you have any left) will be wondering why you don't just dig yourself a nice can of worms and get on with it.

To me, a good pond is one that is either effectively wild or does a decent impression of wildness through management. If you're just fishing and don't know the history of the place, you shouldn't be able to tell the difference.

I used to fish a private lake with a friend who belonged to the club that owned it. It was great at first, with lots of chunky brook trout, but then the club members got nervous and started to overmanage it. First they decided there were too many brookies, so they asked people to kill and eat all the big ones—which I have to say was a hell of a lot of fun. Then they took out most of the thick weeds, because they were fouling fishermen's hooks, but that cut down on the population of freshwater shrimp that made the fish grow fat. Then they stocked kamloops rainbows because there weren't enough brookies anymore, then a gazillion fathead minnows to feed the bows, and I forget what all else.

One day my friend said, "You know, as long as I've been fishing this thing, I've never really gotten a handle on it."

I've also fished a few ponds that were put-and-take— that is, big trout were dumped in to be caught almost immediately. They were fun in a cheap-thrills sort of way, but I didn't consider them great ponds. I thought of them as self-service fish markets.

On the other hand, even these commercial joints

amount to water with fish, and in my limited way of viewing reality, that can't be all bad. It's fine to want the best—if only to see what all the excitement is about—but if you can't now and then happily settle for a little less, you're sunk as a human being.

When it comes right down to it, I suspect the best pond management is a matter of benign neglect and patience. You stock the best fish for the water and then sit back to see what happens. My friend from the private lake once said, "All you can really do for your kids is give them good teeth and an education. Then you have to just leave them alone." The guy's kids turned out better than his lake did.

My friends and I did a lot of pond fishing last season. It was an unusually wet late winter and spring here in northern Colorado, lasting well into June with three times the normal snowpack and lots of rain—twenty-six straight days of it at one point. There were floods and mud slides, mountain roads washed out, crops were damaged, calves died of pneumonia overnight, and of course the rivers—even the ones that stayed in their banks— were an unfishable mess. A friend who owns a fly shop said if things didn't clear up soon, he was gonna have to get a worm cooler.

Okay, fine, but life goes on and trout ponds do fish best on dark, rainy days.

There's one about a forty-five-minute drive north of

here that we hit a couple of times. It's operated, almost as an afterthought, by a dude ranch called Sylvan Dale. Mercifully, the tourist trap end of the ranch—with its swimming pools, manicured lawns and western swing music piped in over loudspeakers—is several miles down the road and completely separate from where you fish.

My favorite place there is called the Mother Pond by some of the people who fish it, although I don't think that's its real name. It fits, though. It's the biggest of four spring-fed ponds in that little valley and it holds the biggest trout.

The first time we went up there, in April, the weather was about as miserable as it gets here: damp, overcast and breezy, with snow turning to rain and back again, and it was cold enough to freeze your fly line in the guides. Naturally, there was a glorious midge hatch that lasted nearly all day, complete with lots of very large trout casually working within casting range.

After a few tries I settled on a #20 cream midge pupa fished on a retrieve so slow all it really did was keep the line tight. When trout are boiling and porpoising lazily like that, a fast retrieve usually doesn't work for the simple reason that trout, unlike humans, don't get excited for no reason.

I lost some fish, not so much because they were big—although some of them were—but because the line would sometimes freeze in the guides before I noticed it and because, what with numb fingers and all, it was too much of a production to retie the tippet-to-fly knot after every large fish as you're supposed to. The midge pattern I was fishing is a quick and easy one to tie, and I had a lot of them, so I'd just fish one until I broke it off in a trout and then warm my hands in my armpits until I got enough feeling back to tie on another one.

It was so cold that day that twice the three of us walked away from rising trout to go back to the truck, crank up the camp kitchen and brew coffee to warm us up.

We had so much fun that we went back a week later. The fishing was almost as good, but the weather was so pleasant by comparison that there's no story to tell. It just rained and we caught some fish.

Then one day in mid-May, A.K., Mike Clark and I drove over to Elktrout Lodge near Kremmling, Colorado, to fish some of the ranch ponds that outfit leases and manages for big trout. It was the Wednesday it rained hard from dawn till dusk here along the East Slope (according to one rain gauge, 3 inches fell near my house), and once again, everyone was talking vaguely about the streams flooding. There were official flash-flood watches posted, but there'd been so many of those in the last six weeks that people had begun to ignore them. A neighbor said, "They don't know if it's gonna flood or not. They're just trying to cover their asses if it does."

We were a little apprehensive when we pulled out at 5:30 in the morning in a cold, steady downpour, but it turned out to be one of those charmed days. We drove south to the town of Golden to get on I-70 and made it just before they closed Colorado 93 because of flooding. Then it was nip and tuck between Georgetown and the Eisenhower Tunnel—we were in a four-wheel, slowly dodging dozens of cars and trucks that were stuck in the snow—but we made it to Silverthorne on the West Slope just before they closed the interstate behind us. In the half hour it took us to eat breakfast at a pancake house, the place filled up with frustrated truck drivers who couldn't get over the pass to Denver.

By the time we got down the Blue River to Kremmling we were out on the northwest corner of the storm. The weather was only overcast and cool with just enough of a light drizzle to make you want to wear your rain slicker: the kind of weather that's perfectly comfortable to fish in and, more important, the kind that makes big pond trout stupid.

Around here, early-season trout ponds mean midges and possibly something else: anything from Callibaetis mayflies to damselfly nymphs to backswimmer beetles to leeches, crawdads or fathead minnows. Sometimes the midges act as camouflage. There'll be just enough of a sparse hatch to get some swallows low over the water and make a few fish rise—smaller fish at that—while the bigger trout are deeper, feeding on something different. Once I was standing ankle deep in a pond casting midges to foot-long trout when an enormous rainbow maybe 25 inches long chased a big crawdad right over the toes of my wading boots. Still, the rings of rising trout on a still pond are so beautiful I always have to at least start with dry flies.

That day at Elktrout was typical of the midge-plus-something-else deal. We got a few trout at the surface, but the most and the biggest ate weighted Muddler Minnows and Woolly Buggers cast from shore. We fished until dusk, had great, cheap steak dinners at a bar in Kremmling, and drove home. The mountain roads were plowed clear of snow and the highway down on the East Slope was wet and slippery with mud in places, but no longer flooded.

By the first week in June it was still raining, the rivers were still flooded, and anyone with an opinion was saying the runoff would last at least another six weeks. In desperation, Mike, Ed and I drove the ten hours up to DePuy's spring creek near Livingston, Montana. We figured it was the closest clear, flowing water, including my well, which by then was running a kind of piss yellow from sediment.

There'd been a series of flood watches for the stream across the road from my house, so as a precaution I hauled some bamboo fly rods, books and a few other things that shouldn't get soaked up to the attic before we left, just in case.

My girlfriend Susan had a place to stay on higher ground if it came to that, and I told her, "Now don't feel like you should take any chances to save my stuff."

She said, "Don't worry about that."

Later that day I was standing across the street watching

the creek with my neighbor Herb, one of those old guys in overalls and a baseball cap who've seen it all. He said this one looked like it could be bad, but probably nothing like the big one in the forties that changed the course of the creek and ate his house and all his belongings. Then he said, "But hell, a guy shouldn't have that much stuff that can't get wet anyway."

The spring creek fished well, considering that it was between hatches, but we got some of our best fish in a couple of the big ponds along there. Okay, technically they're probably "pools," because they have a slow, oily current running through them, but a fisherman defines the character of water by how it's fished. At some point a pool gets big and slow enough to become a pond, although I wouldn't argue about where that point is.

In the evenings we'd go back to the truck, take a coffee break and trade our light dry-fly rods for seven weights and streamers. Then we'd go to one of the ponds, fish the edges first and then make long casts with Woolly Buggers out to where the larger trout were lying along the edges of the almost imperceptible current.

These were the same big browns and rainbows that, by day, would feed with insane precision on infinitesimal midges that looked like pepper spots on the water if you could see them at all. Usually they'd spook at your best cast, and even when they didn't they'd refuse your tiniest flies. They'd be doing that at dusk, too, but the darker it got the more likely they were to forget their spring-creek reticence long enough to wolf a size-4 streamer.

In three days we got enough of a fix to last us a while, and the drive back—going a bit over the speed limit as one is always tempted to do in Wyoming—took the regulation ten hours. There's a time warp up there south of Buffalo somewhere. You can go 120 the whole way and it will still take ten hours.

Back home the sun was shining and the well-watered foothills vegetation was as lush and green as I've ever seen it. The stream out front was high and muddy, but it was still in its banks, and Susan and my house were still there. Not long afterward, we learned that the dike between DePuy's and the Yellowstone River had burst and the spring creek had flooded.

Chapter 12

Second Nature

LAST summer I spent a lot of time exploring some fishing spots near where I live: a few places that were actually new to me and some others I'd just neglected. It turned out to be a good year for it. The runoff was moderate for a change, and the streams were in especially good shape from the end of June on.

Also, for reasons I won't bore you with, I did a lot of

traveling early in the season that had nothing to do with fishing. It had to be done, and some of it wasn't even all bad, but it was nonetheless out in the big bad world where people rush like hell to get to places they don't want to be, where sales of Prozac are at an all-time high and where basically everyone seems to spend their days pissing up a rope.

On a fishing trip you can pass through some places like that, but when that's where you're actually going, it can get grim. Anyway, I ended up getting on way too many airplanes without a rod case and a duffel bag, and by midsummer I'd burned myself out on traveling very far from home.

Looking back on it now, it was a clear message: I'd been wanting to snoop around my own county more than I'd been able to do in the last few years, the fishing was good, and I was fried on traveling anyway. So what more did I want, an engraved invitation?

Not that staying around home is much of a hardship when home is in northern Colorado, in the East Slope foothills of the Rocky Mountains. I've lived and fished in this neighborhood since the early seventies, it's kept me busy and interested for all that time, and by now I know it pretty well, but there are still a handful of public waters I haven't been to, not to mention plenty of places I haven't been *back* to in a decade or more. There's an awful lot of water within day-trip range of my house—hundreds and hundreds of miles of it—and, although none of it is exactly unknown or unfished, there's a lot of it that's overlooked and gets damned little pressure.

I try to remind myself of that whenever I get to complaining about our declining and overcrowded fisheries. After all, most of them are declining because they're crowded, and they're crowded because they're on the short list of places where everyone goes. You know, the spots that are already at least locally famous, the ones they'll tell you about down at the fly shop even if you *haven't* just spent five hundred dollars.

I don't mean to say there aren't problems or that I've given up on trying to help come up with some of the solutions. It's just that, as Edward Abbey once said, you should fight the good fight, but also save part of yourself for pure enjoyment. If you don't, you can become a cynical old shit, as some say Abbey himself did once he stopped taking his own advice.

Of course even in his worst moods, Abbey had a fine sense of guerrilla theater, as when he said the solution to overgrazing on public land was to turn the cattle loose and let people hunt them. Still, you have to enjoy what you're fighting for if only so you don't lose the will to fight. I know I have a tendency to turn sour, so I enjoy what's left if only so I don't crack under the combined weight of what's been lost. My plan is to stay happy even if it fucking kills me.

I spent a lot of time fishing the lower forks of the creek that flows past my house, because I'd neglected them over the last few seasons and also because the Division of

Wildlife hadn't stocked hatchery rainbows in them for a couple of years.

That's because of whirling disease. After several seasons of knowingly stocking whirling-disease-infected rainbows all over the state—for reasons that have never really been explained—the DOW finally decided that was probably not such a good idea after all, so their current policy is *not* to stock infected fish in uninfected waters, although of course by now there are a lot fewer uninfected waters than there used to be.

(I'm not a fisheries biologist—just a lifelong fisherman—but I agree with critics of that policy who say not stocking infected trout is the right thing to do, but why wait till the horses are gone to lock the barn door?)

Anyway, almost all the small streams around here—except those way up in the high country—have populations of brown trout that are the feral descendants of fish stocked decades ago and that are now wild trout in every way that counts. The fisheries biologists I've talked to say browns have more of a resistance to whirling disease than rainbows, cutthroats and brook trout, possibly because browns evolved in Europe, where the parasite came from in the first place, so they've developed a natural immunity. Still, they say browns won't replace rainbows in the numbers we're used to, because they use the habitat differently and there just won't be as many of them.

Well, okay, but I fished some of the streams that weren't stocked with bows, and a lot of the brown trout I caught were bigger and fatter than they'd been in recent years, and although it might just be my imagination, they seemed a little happier, too. I can't help suspecting that's because they weren't competing with truckloads of so-called catchable-sized hatchery fish that look, act and taste like they were stamped out of cat food.

There weren't as many trout in those streams overall, but the browns were bigger, prettier, healthier and more reclusive than the hatchery fish, and because the streams weren't stocked, a lot of fishermen assumed the fishing was no good, so I had more water all to myself.

And after all, these small, fast, freestone creeks aren't *supposed* to have dozens of trout in every pool. This kind of water has an inherent character that it seems to want to return to as soon as it's left alone. As near as I can tell from a little research and some local oral history, back in the days when these were wild cutthroat streams, they were very much like they were that summer: If you went about it right, you'd catch some nice fish, but you wouldn't get a dozen out of every pool.

This is a case in point: We all have to fight the honest fight against whirling disease and fisheries managers who are asleep at the wheel, not to mention dewatering, pollution, development, overpopulation and all the other things that could eventually kill what sometimes seems like the last good way of life. But if, in the aftermath of one of the skirmishes, there happen to be some larger-than-usual brown trout in some local streams that most fishermen aren't bothering with, it can't hurt the cause to go catch a few, can it?

———

I also went up and looked at a place I've been hearing about for a couple of years now and had started to get pretty curious about. There's a high mountain reservoir on the eastern edge of the neighborhood wilderness area that a friend said had some nice beaver ponds full of brook trout on its upstream end. The guy hasn't been there himself in years, but he said he remembered fishing them as a kid.

So Mike Clark and I drove up there to check it out. The reservoir is behind one of those turn-of-the-century earthen dikes that make what they euphemistically call an "enhanced" natural lake. We hiked around to the back side and found the exact spot where the trail petered out. There was a break in the spruce and fir forest with a postcard view of the Continental Divide stretching off to the south, but any tourist who took even two steps out into the boggy beaver meadow would get his $300 running shoes all muddy.

Clearly there had been a good string of beaver ponds through there once, but by now they're mostly either blown out or silted in and well on their way to becoming first bog, then meadow and then woods. In a few places the seeping little watercourse had reestablished itself between narrow banks, but you could still see the pond-shaped patch of grass and spruce seedlings and a few bleached sticks from the old dam sticking out of the ground like ribs.

We slogged around back in there for quite a while looking for the newest ponds, sometimes sinking up to our knees in gooey peat. You could see that twenty or thirty years ago it had probably been downright glorious, but the beavers had done their best decades ago and had long since moved on. We finally caught a few small, jewel-like brookies out of one pond that still had a deep end and a head of water running through it, marveled at the god-awful toughness of these little fish and then hiked out.

It's an article of faith among anglers that there's no such thing as a wasted fishing trip. The two best parts of that one were, our curiosity was finally satisfied and we got to tell our friend that his memory was probably accurate enough, but that he was so damned old it stretched back to a previous geologic era.

On the drive home that day Mike and I passed a little creek that flows under an old Civilian Conservation Corps bridge on the county road, got to talking about it and realized neither of us had ever fished it downstream from there. Within sight of the bridge, it drops down a steep gorge that continues for several miles before it levels out again, and we'd always figured the going would be too rough and there wouldn't be many good pools anyway, so we'd just never bothered with it.

I said, "Why don't we come back tomorrow and fish it?"

Mike said, "Can't," which I took to mean he probably did want to fish it, but the rod orders were piling up as usual and it's hard to write off two days in a row as testing and research. (When you're good friends with a one-syllable conversationalist, you learn to fill in a lot of blanks.)

So the next day I drove back up there by myself and hiked in. A pretty good trail went down a quarter mile or so to a flat spot with a fire ring and the remains of an old woodsy, the kind of party where many beers were drunk and then the empty cans were shot full of holes and left. Below that little bench of land, the canyon narrowed and plunged down steeply. The trail ended right there as abruptly as the one at the edge of the bog had the day before.

There were stretches down there steep enough to make me step sideways and use one hand to brace myself against boulders, and then patches of deadfall I had to climb over and through. Farther up the slope on either side of the streambed it was all second-growth pine forest with a floor of either dry gravel or pine duff, but down along the creek were tangles of willow, dogwood and bigtooth maple, and right along the water, damp, brilliant ferns and moss: a three-foot layer of cool humidity in an otherwise semi-arid landscape.

A lot of the stream was unfishable white water, and sure enough, the good-looking pools and slicks were few and sometimes far between and the going was pretty slow. A few times I had to climb the slope to make any kind of headway at all, and then scrambling down to some of the best spots I was *that close* to having to hold the rod in my teeth so I could use both hands. I'd figured on this from looking at a topo map the night before, so I was traveling pretty light: lunch, sweater, rain slicker and canteen in a day pack, plus the fly rod and one small box of flies.

It had started out bright and sunny that day, but by early afternoon the sky had clouded up and turned cool and rainy—good weather for hard hiking. A few times over the next couple of hours the rain got heavy enough that fish couldn't see a dry fly on the surface, and when that happened I'd hunker down in my rain slicker in the driest spot I could find, and for twenty or thirty minutes at a time, just sort of groove on the concept of waterproofing.

I caught exactly five trout in there: three browns, a rainbow and a brookie, all fat and over a foot long, all on the same #14 yellow caddis dry fly. The biggest was the brook trout—14½ inches. I could think of half a dozen fishermen who'd say that was too far to go and too much trouble for that many trout, but then those are precisely the guys I wouldn't tell about a little patch of overlooked wild stream with no trail and a handful of nice fish.

In fact, I had to stop and wonder if I'd tell *anybody.* After all, wasn't it Lao Tzu who said, "Those who say do not know; those who know do not say"? He's remembered as the great Chou Dynasty Chinese philosopher, but apparently he was also a fisherman.

I knew I'd have to let Mike in on it. When I hadn't showed up for coffee that day, he'd have known where I went. The next time I went into his shop he'd look up from his workbench and ask, "So?" and I knew I wouldn't be able to look him in the eye and say, "Didn't even get a strike."

In the end, I told Mike, A.K., Pat, Mike Price and the rest of that small group of close friends every fisherman has: the ones you spill the beans to about almost everything, and who usually return the favor. I didn't do that right away, though. I kept it to myself for a few days, just to savor the secrecy of it.

I don't know how far down there I went—maybe not as far as it seemed—but I stopped just as the little canyon began to bench out and the walking got a little easier. I guess I didn't want to go so far that I'd come out the other side onto a cabin or a road or a power line, or more likely, a narrow foot trail working its way up from the bottom end. When I thought I'd seen enough, I climbed to the top of the nearest ridge and followed it back to the west through pine woods that seemed as open as a park.

That ridge branched a few times, but I kept the sound of the creek off my left shoulder and came out right at the truck—I mean not so much as two feet off one way or the other. As I was breaking down my rod I realized I'd pulled the pickup down a dirt track and then nosed it into a stand of trees so it was completely hidden from view from the county road. I didn't remember doing that, but by now I guess it's just second nature.

Chapter 13

The Fly Box

L A S T winter, looking forward to the coming season as a fly-fisher tends to do, I started assembling a small-stream fly box.

Another one, that is. I've actually done this five or six times over the years, but the same thing always happens: I put together a tight, no-nonsense little fly selection that's aimed at small mountain creeks, that fits in a single box—

and that works, too—but then slowly, over time, it begins to ooze over into other boxes with more flies in them until eventually I'm back to wearing the full fly vest again.

Not that there's anything wrong with my vest. In fact, I love the thing: It's old, comfortable, and better stocked than some fly shops and I've lugged it on some great trips over the years. It's also as cluttered as a familiar kitchen where, although you don't know precisely where everything is, you still end up looking in the right drawer nine times out of ten. It's just that the vest is one more large item filled with many more small items, and when you're fishing a small, remote trout stream on foot, you want to pare down your gear about as far as it will go.

For me, that's part efficiency and part aesthetics. An unencumbered fisherman can hike farther and cover more water, but there's also something simple and even innocent about the small trout streams I fish in the Rockies, and I feel that if I attack them with too much modern fly-fishing technology, I've sort of missed the point.

I do that: I let things get complicated and end up missing the point. In a way it's just something that happens, but in another way it's the story of my life, and to be honest, fly-fishing hasn't been the worst of it.

The problem is, I admire simplicity in all things, but I also have a bad jones for detail. (Luckily, I also enjoy a good paradox now and then, so this doesn't exactly haunt me.) Anyway, a worldview like that slops over into everything else—love life, politics, fly-fishing—and it's easy to upset the balance. I mean, *enough* fly tackle acts like a door, while too much can become a wall. Never mind about love and politics.

Aside from the fly box—or boxes, as the case may be—I have all my other small-stream tackle trimmed down to what I think of as a lean, bare minimum: rod, reel, hip boots, leader spools, clippers, fly dope. In a medium-sized day pack—a leather-bottomed Hine Snowbridge someone just told me is now a collector's item—I carry the rest of the essentials, like a wool sweater and a rain slicker for the goofy mountain weather, an empty canteen with water purification tablets (to keep the weight down), matches, emergency fire-starting kit, knife, lunch and a coffeepot.

If you compared that to the literal handful of stuff my friend Dave Hughes carries on small streams, you'd have to assume that either he fishes these things like a monk or I fish them like a sultan, although you *could* just figure it's a matter of personal style and leave it at that.

Dave would probably say my coffeepot is a needless extravagance, and he'd be right—from his point of view. But I've found that many of my small-stream expeditions amount to excuses to stage an elaborate coffee break in a stunningly beautiful place miles from the nearest road, which makes the coffeepot as crucial as the fly rod.

It's a fairly large pot, but it's aluminum, so it's light, and other things fit neatly inside it, so it doesn't add any volume. I usually even carry a spare cup in case I attract a guest. On most of my small-stream trips I go to some lengths to be alone—or with the kind of friend who'll go off by himself for hours at a time—but I've noticed that nothing will make a strange fisherman appear out of nowhere like the smell of fresh coffee brewed over a twig fire. Balanced against hospitality, a spare tin cup doesn't weigh that much.

By late last summer, my most recent small-stream selection had, once again, completely dissolved into the full catastrophe, and I did most of my creek fishing with no vest but with three or four fly boxes stuffed in a big side pocket of the pack. It was a compromise and it actually worked okay, except every time I wanted to change flies I had to put down the rod and take off the pack.

I know, that doesn't sound like a big deal, and yes, there are days on some of those streams when I'll fish the same dry fly until I lose it or it falls apart. But still, as a late-twentieth-century fly-fisher, I picture myself as, among other things, a mobile fly-changing unit, and wading to the bank, leaning the rod against a tree and digging into the pack felt clunky and awkward.

It also worked okay in that I had all the flies I needed, but then I also had a lot of flies I *didn't* need, and that seemed sloppy and inefficient on top of clunky and awkward; like I was hiking five miles so I could fish alone, only to get in my own way once I was there. I caught fish, but I guess that wasn't exactly the point.

The flies in all my other small-stream selections had been gleaned from the five or six boxes that live permanently in my vest, plus some others that stay in a drawer except for special occasions, and I think that's where they all went as well: back into those other boxes as the flies dwindled during the season and I was too busy or too lazy to re-tie them.

Not that I'm complaining. If that didn't happen, it would mean I wasn't fishing enough.

Anyway, this last time I tied all the small-stream flies fresh (even though many of them were duplicates), and I allowed myself no more than four of any one pattern in any one size. I figured if you lose four identical flies in a single day on the stream, you're either having such a good day of fishing you should quit while you're ahead, or you're casting so badly you should reel in and go home.

I decided to tie no more flies than would fit in a 4¾-by-3½-inch aluminum Wheatley box. That was the biggest fly box I could find that would fit in the breast pocket of a standard canvas shirt, but it was still small enough to keep me from getting too technical.

On heavily fished spring creeks and tailwaters, where trout feed on blanket hatches and where they're trained by thousands of fly-fishers every season to be damned careful what they eat, you *may* actually need six or eight fly patterns to imitate the different stages and postures of a single bug. I don't mind that. In fact, I like the meticulous fishing, and as a fly tier, I enjoy having an ongoing excuse to tie more and more flies.

At least I like it when I'm in certain moods. In other moods I'll complain about what's happened to the sport; about how on many of our best rivers it's now grand-master chess where not that long ago it was checkers out on the back porch; and about how that, along with the crowds, has killed some of the old charm at the same time it's made us all better fishermen.

Chapter and verse on the small, lesser-fished freestone streams is, there are fewer insects overall than on a spring creek or tailwater, but there are more different kinds, so the trout are hungrier, more curious and more aggressive; wilder, even though they many not be native. These are the places where, as Ed Engle says, "All that stuff from the old fishing books still works." And because your typical small-stream trout aren't large, and because they're not stacked in every pool like cordwood, most of the headhunters and fish counters stay away. That's probably why some of my friends and I get so sentimental about small streams. We think they're the way fly-fishing should be, and that makes them sort of a benchmark.

Apparently there are others who feel that way, too. Just in the last few weeks I've read stories by three writers I admire—Tom McGuane, Steve Bodio and Dave Hughes—all talking about small streams or, as McGuane says, "second-class waters." The stories were all as different as you'd expect them to be, but they all at least hinted at the idea of finding *fishing*, as opposed to what fishing has become.

What it's become, in one view, is a gonzo, technological business where size and numbers are everything, where fly rods are seen as weapons instead of instruments, where crowds are common and large, where courtesy is unknown or poorly understood and so on.

Okay, but then another view is this: I know lots of fly-fishers, and precious few of them are actually like that. Also, I've been gonzo enough myself at times—and I still have it in me—and I love big, fat trout as much as the next guy.

I really do love them, and if there were small, quiet, uncrowded streams around here with hook-jawed torpedoes in them instead of the usual 8- to 12-inchers, those are the ones I'd be fishing. But there aren't, unless you count the odd private club or pay-to-fish joint. Those can be okay now and then, but they're still not the same as the free public water you sniff out on your own. I mean, buying good fishing isn't exactly like paying for sex, as some claim, but it's not entirely *un*like it, either.

But the real lessons of fishing are the ones that come after you've caught some fish. They have to do with things like solitude, quietude, patience, perspective, humor and the sublime coffee break. The kind of person who's a good fly-fisher—though he's not naive—knows that bitchiness and cynicism dishonor the sport as much as headhunting and fish hoggery.

Maybe it's just an age thing. I know young fly-fishers whose only problem with the sport is scraping together enough gas money and time off to fish a fraction as much as they'd like to. I was like that myself not too long ago, and it wasn't all bad. There were frustrations, but they seemed temporary.

By now there are places I've fished in the past that I'm

afraid to go back to for fear of what may have happened there—what probably *has* happened—but then I've heard the same thing from older fishermen all my life and I guess it's just getting to be my turn to pass on that old tradition.

Basically I just want to be a good fly-fisherman, which in these times means being a realist as well as a poet, but a poet nonetheless: voting for this, supporting that, writing letters—sometimes angry ones—speaking up on matters of etiquette, fishing crowded rivers only on days when you're up to it, trying to take carp seriously, searching out the quiet backwaters and in the end stringing up your rod with a glad heart.

That's important because, like it or not, we live like we fish and vice versa. For some of us that's a blessing and for others it's a curse.

Which brings me back to simplicity. I admire it, as I said, and I think I understand that it's not just a matter of neatness and control. Just the opposite, in fact: Ways of life that ignore the headlong, chaotic, messy character of things end up looking more like simplemindedness than enlightenment. I guess when it comes right down to it, the true nature of simplicity is pretty damned complicated.

There was surprisingly little agony to selecting which flies to tie for the small-stream box. I just pictured the creeks I fish most often, summoned the confidence I have about them and let the fly patterns come out of my head on their own. After all, there are only a few things I really know how to do well, but one of them is how to fish small, pocket-water trout streams in the Rocky Mountains.

I ended up with eighty flies in fourteen patterns, heavy on the dry flies and mostly on size-14 and -16 hooks. That's more flies than some people I know would need, but they still didn't completely fill the little fly box, which I thought was a nice touch. I won't list the patterns because that would sound like a mail-order catalogue pitch: "These patterns have been shown to be the most effective after exhaustive testing by our staff of small-stream experts."

It's more like they were chosen spontaneously—after a casual meditation exercise—by a single, opinionated fisherman who continues to use bamboo fly rods and still believes that there's more voodoo than science to catching trout. For me, they're close to perfection; for you, they wouldn't stink, but flies of your own choice would probably work better.

But I will tell you about one. It's a dry fly called the McGuane, as described by its inventor Tom McGuane in his book *Live Water.* It sounded pretty in print. I tied one and it *was* pretty, so I added it to the box for literary reasons. It was a great book, so it must be a great fly, right? I guess that's what I mean by voodoo.

Of course now I have to resist the temptation to change one little snippet of something on the pattern and rename it the *Improved* McGuane, but that's my problem.

Chapter 14

McCook

LAST January, toward the end of the season, Steve Peterson, his dog Poudre and I spent a few days pheasant hunting in the neighborhood of McCook, Nebraska. This is generally known—among those who insist on rating such things—as a good, though not quite blue-ribbon area, and that's what we like about it. There are usually enough birds to go around, but later on in the season at least, it's not particularly crowded, and I don't detect many symptoms of the love/hate relationship local citizens can develop when large numbers of tourist hunters or fishermen descend on them.

That is, I don't think they love us or anything, but they don't seem to hate us either, or even to mind us being around—further evidence that humans of any persuasion are best taken in small doses.

The weather that week was classic Great Plains winter: wet, cold, snowy, foggy, slippery and bitter. You have to be a native-born Midwesterner like I am to appreciate it. This is the weather and the country that created the American frontier consciousness, at least among those who survived prairie madness. "It ain't fit out there for man nor beast" is what they used to say about it when I was a kid. And then they'd bundle up and go out in it.

I guess the hunting was poor that week if you go by numbers of birds bagged, but then Steve and I agree that's the simple-minded short view, even if those who shoot better think differently. The fact is, over time a life frittered away in the pursuit of sport makes perfect sense, but no one trip tells the whole story, and endless successes without a little failure and hardship would probably get boring.

It was fairly miserable to be out slogging the fields knee-deep in wet snow and hoarfrost; Steve referred to one day's hunt as a "death march." On the other hand, hoarfrost is quite beautiful and you don't usually get to see it by staying inside. There was almost no one else out there—no farmers and only two or three other hunters—and we saw hundreds of pheasants, although precious few of them were roosters and all but a handful flushed wildly and far out of range.

Everyone says cold and snow are supposed to bunch the birds up and make them hold better, which is why we went out there when we did, but that old saw is less and less true as you get on into the season, and every pheasant between Chicago and Denver learns that humans with dogs and shotguns mean them no good. By Christmas, it's possible to flush every pheasant in a field just by slamming your car doors.

Of course it's not like that early in the season, but then we usually manage to miss the first half of it altogether because you can still catch trout on dry flies back home in Colorado.

As it turned out, we got a few birds on a trip that could easily have been a complete bust in terms of meat, and otherwise just enjoyed kicking around on the Great Plains for a few days.

McCook is the kind of small Middle American city where you can find a cheap motel patronized mostly by truckers and hunters at this time of year—complete with a garbage pail and a yard light out back for cleaning birds—a quiet little bar off Main Street that serves a great steak dinner special and a breakfast joint where the farmers hang out and where the waitresses ask you how the hunting has been without first having to ask what you're doing in town.

It's hard not to overhear snatches of conversation in a place like this, and I'm always struck by a certain sensible outlook I've come to miss here in the People's Republic of Boulder County, Colorado, which is a hell of a lot less rural than it was when I moved here almost thirty years ago.

(I don't mean that Colorado has gone completely to hell, it's just that there are a few too many people around now who moved out west so they could live on a dirt road, only to spend all their time bitching about the dust.)

You see, urban folk somehow assume that things are supposed to go perfectly for them at all times: schedules must be met, expectations must be fulfilled, comfort must be maintained. Consequently, they're aggravated beyond all reason by any little mistake or delay. But rural people understand that life is basically a dangerous, unmanageable mess, so when things go wrong, their suspicions are confirmed and it's just a blessing no one was killed. When things occasionally go right, they're delighted. Whatever happens, they have a comfortable grasp on reality, not to mention an ironclad work ethic.

"Well," a guy will say as he stands up from his third cup of coffee, "I won't get it done sittin' here."

He's right. It's ten degrees out, the sun is nearly up and the morning is half gone already.

So we hunted hard and got a few birds. Typically, I missed what should have been an easy shot with both barrels and then made a hard one because it happened quickly and I didn't have time to stew about it. Poudre, Steve's little Llewellen setter, worked well and made some pretty points, even though she does have that hardheaded streak and Steve had to yell at her a couple of times. But then I've never been hunting with these two when they didn't have a little spat. Luckily, neither of them is the type to hold a grudge.

To a dog owner, hunting is a whole different business. It's training and the rewards of training; an occasion for pride or despair, but either way it's all about how the dog does. To the dog, it's the meaning of life itself, however it turns out. Happiness comes when both the human and the dog arrive at the same vision of success.

I don't know much about dog training, but I've been around hunting dogs most of my life, and in the last few years I've gone on some training sessions with Steve and Poudre. He works the dog, I shoot the birds. Somebody has to do it.

Poudre is coming along, which is what you say about all but the most hopelessly idiotic dogs. She retrieves well now, but for a couple of seasons she'd find your bird, pick it up, look back at you and then spit it out as if to say, "You shot it, you carry it." Steve hated that, but I always thought it was kind of charming.

I really only know two things about training a hunting dog: One is that a human and a dog work well together to the extent that the human understands dogs. The other is that even a good dog breaks your heart for four or five years until it gets good, then has a few prime seasons, then it begins to get old, slow and arthritic and breaks your heart all over again.

I've known men who couldn't always recall their first ex-wife's name, but who would weep openly at the memory of a good dog that's been dead for twenty years.

But I still enjoy the company of most dogs more than that of most people, because dogs are capable of uncomplicated enthusiasm. Like every hunting dog I've ever known, Poudre goes headlong all day whether there are a hundred birds or none at all, and then falls into a wet pile. When we sneak her into the motel room at night, one of us usually has to carry her like a thirty-pound sack of potatoes.

Steve has hunted a lot around McCook and has some local contacts, but we also just stopped and asked to hunt on a few places. (There are still parts of America where you can ask a stranger for a small favor and he's likely to say, "Sure, go ahead," instead of calling the cops.) We're both shy about doing this, but Steve is usually the one to go knock on the door, because he's a little more presentable than I am, or at least after a few days of hunting he looks a little less like he spent the night before under a bridge. It seems to work. He gets permission more often than not.

One day when Steve was knocking on a kitchen door, I sat in the pickup having a detailed flashback: It was 1964 and my long-lost friend Jack Darrow and I were driving west across the country in an elderly Volkswagen. We'd left Ohio on a journey of three thousand miles without enough gas money to get us out of the state, assuming we'd be able to just work our way along. And we did. There were some ups and downs, but through the rural parts of Michigan, Wisconsin, Minnesota, North Dakota, Montana, Idaho and Washington, there were kind folks who gave us a few dollars and maybe a meal for some chores that probably didn't really need doing. By the look of us, they probably understood that we were on our way to Haight-Ashbury for some serious debauchery, but they could also see that we were broke, willing to work and proud enough that we'd sooner steal than beg. I never felt more at home among strangers.

One morning outside McCook we spent half an hour talking about the price of pigs and corn with a farmer who let us hunt on his place. He said things weren't going well, but, honestly, they seldom *did* go well and he'd sort of gotten used to that.

I said I'd never understood why farmers weren't rich. "After all," I said, "you guys produce the one product everyone needs to live."

He looked at me like I was from Mars, which I might as well have been, but I wasn't kidding. I really don't get it. Finally I said, "Well, if I ever figure it out, I'll call you."

He grinned and said, "You do that."

It's a fair bargain, I guess. Steve and I get a nice long walk and a few pheasants. The farmer gets a story that'll crack 'em up down at the café.

We did get pretty wet and cold on that trip, and on the afternoon of the last day Steve piled full stride into a hidden strand of barbed wire and injured his knee. He went down hard and I didn't like the look on his face when he landed. Even Poudre came back and whined at him once before she went off to look for more pheasants.

While he lay there deciding how badly he was hurt, I looked back across the field toward the truck. It couldn't have been less than a mile away and I started to think what you have to think at a moment like that: That's a long way to carry two shotguns, a couple of dead birds and a grown man, but it would probably be better than leaving him and going for help. The day was wet, windy and bitter—real frostbite weather; there wasn't much in the way of shelter and no wood for a fire. However long it would have taken me to hike out, drive to town and then lead someone back would have been too long.

Maybe I could put the truck in four-wheel and drive out here to get him, but then if I got stuck we'd really be screwed.

Sometimes when you're hunting or fishing you realize you could be right up against it, that you'll probably have to do something quickly and that the right thing to do is also the hardest. I guess I'd just rediscovered the Protestant Ethic.

Back at the warm, dry, cozy café, anyone you put this

to would agree. "Yup, it wouldn't be easy, but you'd have to try and carry him out." They wouldn't be surprised at the question, either. After all, life is a dangerous, unmanageable mess. Even someone who can't understand the economics of farming should know that.

I'd just about decided on the good old over-the-shoulder fireman's carry when Steve got to his feet and brushed himself off. I was glad to hear it when he said nothing was broken and he could walk.

We left a little early that afternoon, more because of an ice storm that was blowing in than because of Steve's knee. He was only limping a little bit and said as long as he kept moving it wasn't too bad. But the dirt county roads were creased with snowdrifts and slick in the bare spots, and the paved highway was worse.

We took 34 West slowly, slowing down even more every time we passed another car in the ditch. The cab was filled with the aroma of truck-stop coffee and the faint odors of a few dead pheasants and a wet dog. Poudre was curled in a ball with her nose under her tail, sleeping every bit as hard as she'd hunted. In the end the five-hour drive back to Colorado took more like seven or eight hours, part of which we filled up with Steve's collection of great old blues tapes. We covered the fifty miles between Benkelman and Wray wondering if Howlin' Wolf used sophisticated phrasing or just had a lousy sense of rhythm.

And then there was the usual talk of other hunts, other dogs and other shotguns. I've noticed that hunters are always vaguely in the market for a new shotgun, even though the old ones work just fine and what they could really use is more practice. As a friend of mine likes to say, "If you can't hit, the solution probably ain't a bigger gun."

For some reason, the shotgun business takes on extra weight during and after hunts like this one. I know in my heart that nothing can be done when the birds are spooky from several months of hunting, but I still somehow suspect that if I was carrying a $6,000 Italian sidelock 16-gauge double, they'd flush in range.

And yes, that long dead stretch between the end of pheasant season and the beginning of fishing is a dangerous time. On any given day a guy could be in town doing errands and decide to drop by the gun shop just to browse casually among the fowling pieces.

The morning after we got back I called Steve to see how his knee was. Better, he said. As soon as the swelling goes down, we should probably go back. After all, there are still a few weeks left in the season.

Chapter 15

Taking It Personally

I'VE been fishing this little trout stream off and on for as long as I've lived here, which by now feels like forever. I could say I learned how to fish for trout here and not be far wrong. I've seen it in all of its moods and all of mine. I've spent time on it with old friends who are no longer alive. I guess you could say I've gotten a little sentimental about it.

At one time or another I've probably claimed to have fished it "hundreds of times," which is the kind of exaggeration any fly-fisher will understand: It means it's close to home, small, quiet, pretty, and generous with its medium-sized trout. It also means I won't tell you where it is.

Ed Engle once wrote of another little trout stream, "It was the kind of secret fishing spot we all have: so intimate you question taking even your closest friend to it, not because he might blab the location all over town, but because if he doesn't like it you'll take it personally."

I've fished in a lot of other places—sometimes for much larger trout—but I still like coming home to a small, familiar stream. For one thing, the pressure's off. There's no stewing about how far you've traveled, how much you're paying the guide or how the guys in the next boat are doing; no wondering how the fish would taste if you dared to kill one, because over the years you've eaten a few dozen of these. They were good. You just go to a place you know of that would be worth the hike just for the view (although you'd never think of going there without a fly rod), slide into it at your own pace and let your mind turn inward. Or maybe it's outward: whichever way your mind goes while the rest of you is fishing.

I can usually get packed in about ten minutes, because there are no real decisions to make. I know I'll take hip boots instead of chest waders, the one small-stream fly box, a handful of odds and ends (clippers, a few leader spools, fly floatant), lunch, coffeepot and a favorite 7½-

foot, 5-weight bamboo rod that a wine connoisseur friend once called, "An impertinent little fly rod with amusing pretensions." I'm an equipment freak from way back, so I may *want* more gear than that, but by now I know this is all I'll actually *need.*

Oh yeah, and I always check my leader, running my fingers along the monofilament from where it's attached to the fly line, down the taper to the light tippet section that I'll tie the fly to, looking for wind knots, nicks or abrasions that make for weak spots. That's a small but necessary ritual, and I do it at home now because I know I won't think of it on the water—at least not until I set the hook on a good fish and break the leader.

The last time I fished this stream was back in late August. At just over 9,000 feet in the Colorado Rockies, that amounts to the beginning of autumn and the height of dry-fly season. On that particular day, the falls seemed like a good place to start, not just because it's a gorgeous spot, but also because under that little cascade is the biggest, deepest pool on the stream.

In the past, you had to stumble upon these falls by accident as you worked your way up the stream—and the first time you saw them your heart would jump in your chest. But then last summer the Forest Service put up a sign along the old logging road pointing out the spot. A week or so later, a local fisherman pulled it down. No, it wasn't me, but I think I know who it was and I approve. Some things are best left as they are, to be discovered in the normal course of events, and even a fat-assed bureaucrat who never leaves the office has to know that the quickest way to trash a pretty little out-of-the-way spot is to put up a goddamned sign.

When I got there that day I found that the sign had been put back up, probably by an FS trail crew with time on its hands. I don't know, maybe it's harmless. The falls are a bit of a hike off the four-wheel-drive track and so far there's no trail beaten down there. And both the road and the stream are not much traveled.

I decided to think about it later, hiked down to the falls, found a convenient flat rock and sat down to watch the pool.

When I first started fly-fishing, I noticed that a lot of the older guys would do this: Instead of wading right in and starting to cast, they'd hunker down and study the water for a while, maybe taking a long time to load and stoke up a pipe or properly caress and light a cigar. I started doing that because they did it, and it wasn't easy at first, but I eventually realized it can take ten minutes to spot something like the subtle rise of a nice trout in the shade of an overhanging bank—a fish you can spook without ever knowing he was there if you're too eager.

Those old fishermen: They're slow-moving and crabby and some of them talk to themselves, but they can catch trout. I've been studying to become one of them for a long time now, and there are those who'll tell you I've made it. I may not always catch a lot of fish, but just last month I was accused of talking to myself. I said, "We *all* talk to ourselves, we just don't all move our lips." Anyway, I may be making progress, but I think I have a good decade to go before I'm a bona fide old fart.

There were four rising fish in that pool that I could see: three at the tail of it where the water shallowed up and one in the shade against the far bank. There were some yellow caddis flies on the water, a few big olive mayflies and some smaller, darker mayflies I guessed to be Red Quills.

On another kind of stream—say, a heavily fished spring creek where everyone is dressed like a catalogue model— I'd have had to watch a rising trout long enough to see which bugs he was eating, and if I didn't see a floating fly go down in a swirl, I'd have to figure they were on the mayfly nymphs or caddis pupae just under the surface. If the trout were boiling lazily I'd think they were eating the slow-moving mayfly emergers, but if they were slashing and darting I'd guess it was the more active caddis pupae. No guarantees, of course, just the rule of thumb, some-place to start.

I might even have waded in well downstream of the rising fish to net some insects and see exactly what they looked like. I *have* fooled around with aquatic entomol-ogy a little bit—if you fly-fish long enough it's in-evitable—and I've even read a few fat, dull books about it, but in the long run I think I've learned more with a 50-cent aquarium dip net.

Okay, in a pinch I can do all that, it's lots of fun, and af-ter a few educated guesses, I can sometimes even get it right. But then on a small, lightly fished freestone creek like this the trout aren't usually selective to a single stage in the life cycle of one insect. That doesn't mean the highly technical stuff wouldn't have worked, it's just that some streams are more charitable than others.

And I knew one of the idiosyncrasies of this particular stream is that when there are even a few of those yellow caddis flies on the water, the fish will eat them. That's one of those little bits of regional folklore you'll pick up if you're around long enough and if you're smart enough to listen to those old-timers. It's one of the reasons why locals sometimes really do catch more fish than the tourists.

I tied on a #16 yellow caddis dry fly and started working on the three trout at the tail of the pool, using an across and slightly downstream cast to keep the leader from dragging in the current. I missed one, hooked and landed the second (a chubby 10-inch brown) and spooked the third with all the commotion. Not a bad start.

Then I waded upstream and tried for the fish along the far bank. It took a longer cast with an upstream mend in the line to get a good drift over there, and I practiced that in open water a few times to make sure I had it right before I lengthened the cast to put the fly over the fish.

In the summer at least, there's always a chance that a bank feeder will be eating something other than what the fish out in the more open currents are feeding on (like clumsy ants or beetles that have fallen into the water), but I tried the caddis because that's what I had on, and the fish took it on the third drift. Another little brown.

There were no more rising trout and I'd come to fish

dry flies, so I almost headed upstream. But then sometimes the idea that a deep pool might have a big trout or two feeding in deep water can be too much to resist, so I decided to put in a few minutes of nymph fishing, just out of curiosity.

The choice of a fly pattern for nymphing can seem too huge to comprehend, and I've seen nymph fishers standing like zombies on riverbanks, gazing into open fly boxes, literally frozen by indecision. (I recognize that when I see it because I've done it myself.)

The thing is, aquatic insects spend most of their lives on the stream bottom, where they are regularly eaten by trout. Mayflies and stoneflies have a nymphal stage. These are six-legged, armored bugs that fly-fishers think are handsome but that I heard one nonangler describe as looking like wet cockroaches.

Caddis flies and midges have bottom-dwelling larval stages that turn into pupae before they swim to the surface to hatch into winged flies. Most of the larvae are sort of wormlike, and the pupae look like abbreviated, half-drowned versions of the adults.

When you figure there are several species of each kind of insect in a typical stream—each a different size and color—plus an odd assortment of scuds, sow bugs, cranefly or alder-fly larvae, true aquatic worms or whatever, you're looking at a pretty vast herd of bugs, any one of which could be what the trout are hungry for.

I tied on a #14 Hares Ear nymph on general principles. It's a good, all-round nymph pattern that could pass for a mayfly or smallish stonefly nymph or a caddis pupa, and again, it's a fly that's known to work on that stream. I nipped two small split shot on the leader about 18 inches above the fly and lobbed it into the current up toward the head of the pool, stripping line as it swept back downstream and trying to keep a dead drift.

A few casts later I set up when I thought I saw a slight hesitation in the tip of the floating line, but there was nothing there. Maybe I'd missed a strike, or maybe my split shot had just ticked bottom—as it's supposed to. If your split shot aren't bumping the bottom now and then, you're not fishing deep enough.

Of course, if you *are* fishing deep enough, you're gonna hang up and lose some flies. That's the deal. A couple of bad days in a row can cost you $30 worth of store-bought nymphs and turn you into a dry-fly purist—if the sheer beauty of watching the drift and seeing the strike hasn't done that already—but then a good day makes it all okay again.

After fifteen minutes or so I'd landed one decent brown and a brook trout about as long as my thumb. (Catching a baby trout now and then is always encouraging; it means the stream is healthy and there's another generation of fish coming along.) I could have tried some other nymph patterns or I could have switched to a streamer. Stripping a streamer pattern that imitates a fingerling trout or forage fish through a deep pool is a good way to hang a big fish if there's one there.

It can all work, but when it comes right down to it, how

you fish a piece of water depends as much on your mood as anything else. I reeled in and walked around the falls to where I could fish dry flies in the pocket water upstream.

It was in this water, with its jumbled boulders, braided currents and plunge pools, that I got my first and best lessons in reading a stream. All things being equal, a trout wants to lie in fairly slow-moving water to conserve energy, but he also wants to be close to faster-moving water that carries both nymphs and floating flies. That's more or less true everywhere, but the effect is miniaturized in pocket water, so that a good lie can be not much bigger than the fish that's in it. You look for creases, conflicting currents, back eddies, slicks behind rocks or along fallen logs: anyplace where food-carrying current lies up against holding water.

I kept my casts short, to keep as much line as possible off the water to avoid drag, and since there were places where a good float would only go 6 or 8 inches, I tried to put the fly where I thought a trout would be.

It's a great feeling to cast a fly to a good-looking spot and have a fish take it—makes me feel like I actually know what I'm doing—and when I get a strike from a place where I didn't really expect one, I try to ask myself, What the hell was he doing *there?* I don't mean I have to reach any grand conclusions, it's just that doing that over and over again has begun to give me a sense for where the fish will be—or at least something to base a hunch on.

If I remember right, I was fishing a Royal Wulff, although it could just as easily have been a Hares Ear Parachute. Whatever, it was something nondescript, in about a size 14 or 16 with white hair wings so I could see it in the broken water.

The logic of fly-fishing says that a trout eats your imitation thinking it's a real insect, so it should *look* as much like a real insect as possible. That sounds reasonable, and on the one hand it's absolutely true, but on the other, if it were really that simple, there wouldn't be nearly as many fly patterns as there are.

The trouble is, trout don't always play by the rules, so for every anatomically correct fly pattern that works, there's a corresponding Christmas tree ornament that works, too. Don't ask me why. Those things exist because fly tiers are hopeless tinkerers working with two simple facts: that occasionally someone really does come up with a great new idea and that in the meantime it's pretty hard to tie a fly that *won't* catch a fish sooner or later.

I guess I fish white-winged dry flies in fast water because I can see them and because that's the traditional approach. I have to assume those traditions didn't just come out of thin air, although who really knows? There are fly tiers now who make their wings out of fluorescent orange hair for better visibility. These things are so ugly it's a crying shame to fish them, but they work: proof that trout have no taste. And then there are others who tie the same flies with black wings that they can see against the glare of chromy water. Those work too, and they're a lot prettier.

I covered a lot of water pretty quickly in that stretch,

making a few good casts to each likely-looking spot and then moving on to the next one. I caught mostly brook trout, which I expected. The falls are a natural boundary, with mostly brown trout and a few rainbows below and mostly brookies—and sometimes a few cutthroats—up above.

I didn't catch a lot of trout, but I did lose count, which means I must have caught enough. The first thing you learn is, no matter how hard you fish, you can't catch them all. The second thing you learn is, you'll be a lot happier if your definition of good fishing depends more on poetry than body counts.

By late afternoon I'd come to one of the few flat, slow-flowing meadow stretches on the stream, and instead of just fishing through it and moving on, I sat down on a log. I figured if there was going to be an evening rise, this would be the best place to fish it. And okay, maybe I was a little tired and needed a break.

The evening hatch would probably be blue-winged Olive mayflies or caddis or both, maybe with a fall of Red Quill spinners thrown in, and I knew from experience that even if I fished until full dark I could bushwhack north through the pine woods to the old logging road and grope my way back to the truck. I've done it hundreds of times.

Then again, there are those weird evenings when everything seems right—weather, season, moon phase, whatever—but you can sit there till midnight and not a single trout will rise. It happens.

I thought about hiking back to the big pool under the falls, waiting for full darkness and then swimming a deer-hair mouse though the deepest water: the kind of trick that won't usually get you a fish in a little stream like this but that can sometimes get you one real big one. I'd never caught a trout longer than 14 inches in that pool, but I believed there must be a hog in there.

(I guess it also occurred to me that if a guy was ever going to chain a Forest Service sign to his pickup and rip it out of the ground, right after dark would be as good a time as any to do it. Just an idle thought.)

When it comes right down to it, there are countless fish to catch and almost as many ways to do it with a fly rod, but you can't do it all in one day and too much second-guessing can bring on a panic attack. It's better to just sit on your log and wait for the trout to start rising, and then wait a little longer, because it's usually the smaller ones that start early, while the big fish often wait till the hatch is in full swing.

Meanwhile, you might as well enjoy that view. You know, the one that would have been worth the hike all by itself, even without the fish. Well, okay, maybe not *without* the fish, but what the hell, there you are with time on your hands, and unless you're a stone-cold technician, you have to admit it's pretty cosmic: a small, bright meadow with the white blooms of cow parsnip looking like frost in the afternoon light; beyond that a mixed forest with the lodgepole pine trunks dark in the shade, but the white aspens seeming to glow; and above all that the still snowy crags of the Indian Peaks very close on the western horizon. A raven is honking back in the trees somewhere. Back in town—30-some miles and 3,000 feet downslope—it's a hot day, but up here the air is so clear and cool it almost makes the bridge of your nose hurt.

But then the whole stream is beautiful—every inch of it in its own way—and I do notice, even while I'm fishing. I just don't always think to mention it.

Chapter 16

The Right Thing

LAST summer I spent a few days fishing a river in . . . Well, let's say an unnamed Canadian province. I was in a blue fiberglass Mack boat with a guide named . . .

Okay, maybe I should start somewhere else.

A few days after I got home from that trip, I got a phone call from an outdoor writer whose name you'd surely recognize. He said, "I heard you were up on the Such-and-such River with old What's-his-name."

"Yeah, how'd you hear about that?" I said. "I just got back."

"Oh, everybody around here's talking about it," he said, and before I had time to be flattered he added, "We're a little concerned."

The thing is, this is one of a handful of trout rivers in that part of Canada that are still more or less undiscovered. I mean undiscovered in the modern sense that there are no fly shops in either of the small, nearby towns; the streams aren't on the destination lists of any of the big fly-fishing travel services; some people are licensed by the province to guide on them, but there aren't any full-time operations there—yet. And more to the point, there haven't been any big, full-color, where-to-go-type magazine stories written about them.

I knew that. That's why I wanted to fish there in the first place, and sure enough, it was everything I'd hoped for. The trout were big, healthy, unscarred and not that hard to catch, and there were plenty of them. The river itself was lovely and quiet, with not a beer can and hardly a footprint to be seen. We fished from a drift boat most of the time, and now and then, as we passed a road bridge, we might see a wading fisherman or two (what my guide called "bank maggots"), but we saw none in between, either on shore or in other boats.

People do now and then float this river, but the put-ins and take-outs are rough and improvised, which is always a good sign. Taking the boat out one evening we got the truck and trailer stuck in the mud. It was glorious.

The people I met were laid-back and friendly, and no

one was wearing one of those slightly belligerent T-shirts I've seen in tourist towns that say things like "I'm not *from* anywhere, I live here."

When my friend the guide and I pulled into the first small town, we had a headlight out that we figured we'd better get fixed before we started fishing or it would never get fixed at all. We stopped at a little garage and asked the guy how soon he could get to it. He was up to his elbows in a pickup truck with several other cars waiting, but he glanced out front at the MacKenzie boat we were towing and asked, "Goin' fishin', ey?" We said yes and he said, "Well, then, I'll do it now."

In one sense that's just the way Canadians are, but it's also a sign that the adversarial relationship people inevitably develop with large numbers of visiting fishermen hasn't taken hold yet. That same year I pulled into a gas station in a big-time fishing town here in the U.S. to get a tire patched. I said to the guy, "I'm going fishing, so I'm in kind of a hurry," and he said, "Yeah, who ain't?" In a sense that's just how *Americans* are, but it still makes the point.

All in all, the trip to that Canadian river reminded me of the old days. Or, the memory of a fisherman being what it is, it was like what I *think of* as the old days.

Okay, fine, but the question is, if you write about fishing for a living, do you do a story on a place like that? If so, why? And if not, why not?

The average reader—who's always on the lookout for a

good place to fish—might like to know where this river is. Anyone can understand that. But then anyone can also understand that the relative handful of locals who fish it now are horrified at the idea of that reader—and maybe a few hundred, and then maybe a few *thousand* of his colleagues—learning about the spot.

The guide who took me there could make some money from those new fishermen, but even he was worried. On the drive back he asked me straight out, "Do you think I could ruin this?"

"Probably not all by yourself," I said, "but you could sure contribute." I didn't say it at the time, but I remember thinking, Actually, *I'm* the one who could ruin it.

There *is* money to be made from a good trout river, and this particular one is not in what you could call a rich neighborhood. If the people around there who guide or tie flies or run motels and cafés made a few extra bucks from fishermen, they wouldn't be buying heaters for their swimming pools; they'd be paying the rent and buying groceries.

But then if too many fishermen come—and no one knows beforehand how many is too many—the quality of the fishing begins to decline. Not always right away, maybe not even for a few years, but eventually people start talking about how crowded it's getting and how good the fishing *used* to be.

Granted, special regulations and other management tactics can help if they're instituted soon enough (usually they're not), and some restraint on the part of local guides and outfitters makes a big difference. For instance, when I asked my friend if there were any special regs on that river, he said it didn't matter because "In this boat, the rule is catch and release."

So total ruin isn't inevitable, but it's also true that once a river gets on the circuit, it'll never be the same again. The character of the place will become less rural and blue-collar. There'll be more people wandering around town and more cars on the roads. The old fly patterns won't work as well anymore. Most of the changes will be small in themselves, but add them all up and they make a big difference.

Meanwhile, that restless mob of tourist anglers will still be sniffing around, searching for the great new undiscovered trout stream, because this one isn't quite it anymore. (And I'm one of those fishermen: no less fickle than the worst of them.)

By the time the place is on the map, some new money has come into the little town in question, which may or may not be a good thing in the long run. The people who made that money are probably happy enough, at least for a while, but those who liked the town back when it was small and sleepy probably aren't, nor are the local fishermen, who have had their river clobbered by the tourists.

At its worst, this can start a real class war. Rich tourists begin to want summer places there because it's quiet and sleepy, the fishing is good, and the land is still cheap. They build large, ostentatious houses, preferably along the river, where they promptly close public access. As more and more of them come, the town begins to grow unexpectedly and uncontrollably. (There's a breed of developer that preys on little communities that have never dealt with growth and so don't have a comprehensive plan.) Local services are stretched and taxes go up to pay for improvements. Suddenly what seemed quaint at first begins to look scruffy. A movement begins to turn those muddy old put-ins and take-outs into paved boat ramps with parking lots, picnic tables and solar-powered outhouses.

The place changes, and eventually the local people begin to undergo a strange metamorphosis of their own. In the beginning they're charmingly funky neighbors and characters (the kind you tell funny stories about to your friends back in L.A.), then they become employees, and finally they're seen as an undesirable element.

If you don't believe that, ask a beach bum in Islamorada, Florida, or an old cowboy in Jackson Hole, Wyoming. For the opposing view, ask a real estate agent.

If you happen to be the writer who's credited with getting it all started, there will be those who want to shake your hand and others who'd like to shoot you on sight and feed your carcass to one of the few remaining bears. You could say—rightfully—that it wasn't entirely your fault; that, in fact, you were just a pawn in a chess game involving lifestyle changes, economics, demographics, the population explosion, huge growth in the fly-fishing business and so on. You could even say, just as rightfully, that it would have happened anyway, with or without that one little story you wrote, but you could still either get your hand shaken or your butt fed to the bears.

When it's all said and done, even the fly tiers, shop owners and guides may eventually have some regrets. (Nobody can pine for the old days like an aging guide.) It's easy to be cynical these days, but the fact is, there are extremely few actual environmental rapists in the fly-fishing industry, and even those rare oddballs who have no real love for it realize that if the resource is wrecked they'll have to go back to selling used cars.

If you think the writers themselves are whores, there's probably nothing I can say to change your mind, but I will point out for the record that every fishing writer I've ever talked to does this because he loves the life and the places where wild fish live; and even if he *was* tempted to sell out a place for money, no magazine pays enough.

But the question remains: Do you write the story or not?

It can be an easier decision closer to home. I've written an outdoor column for the local daily newspaper here for the past fifteen years and have lived and fished in the county for considerably longer than that. In that time I've seen a fair number of fisheries go downhill.

One of the places where I used to fly-fish more or less undisturbed for cutthroats and brook trout is now so crowded it's become one of those new National Forest fee areas. I don't think the Forest Service has either the legal or the moral right to charge the public to go on public land, but of course the FS doesn't care *what* I think. I'm currently boycotting the place on principle, but that's not much of a hardship because by now the fishing is pretty lousy anyway.

I never wrote about any of those little lakes and streams up there by name, but I did write some stories about the fishing in the general area—which I thought were vague enough—and those stories did appear at a time when lots of people were moving here. I was never tarred and feathered by local fly-fishers (and I know some who would have done that if they thought it was appropriate), but I can't say I'm entirely blameless, either.

The precious few relatively undiscovered spots still left around here are usually too small and delicate to take the added pressure even a newspaper column could generate, and so I pretty much follow the rule that most outdoor writers go by: If it's already well known and popular, or so remote and expensive to get to that it only sees a handful of fishermen every year, go ahead and write about it. If it's not, write about the fishing in a large chunk of national forest or wilderness area without being too specific, or do a story on mountain lakes or small streams in general, possibly including tips on how one could research these things for oneself.

Sure, maybe there's a little selfishness involved here—I can't deny that—but then when a guy complained to me once about all the columns I'd written about unnamed fishing spots, I said, "I'll make you a deal: You tell me about your favorite secret place, I'll publish its exact location in the newspaper, and then we'll talk."

The fact is, anyone who's been in this business for a

while has probably ruined a couple of once-good fishing holes by writing where-to-go-and-which-rock-to-stand-on stories about them—usually early on before it sinks in that people are actually reading this stuff. I won't tell you about mine because they were a while ago now, so maybe the statute of limitations has run out.

Anyway, it's always the first thing you think about when you sit down at the old word processor. That and accuracy, even though you know that all the available facts laid end to end don't always point to the truth.

In terms of journalistic ethics, you can always invoke the people's right to know and that old premise that all you're supposed to do is tell the story and let the chips fall where they may, but that can easily become a copout. I mean, a public official with his hand in the cookie jar is one thing, while a secluded beaver pond with twenty brook trout that could be fished out in a single afternoon is another.

There are always two sides to it, and that's why both readers and writers will always have mixed feelings about reporting. Thomas Jefferson once said that given the choice between good government and a good newspaper, he'd take the newspaper. Much later in life he said that you shouldn't read newspapers at all because it's better to be ignorant than misinformed.

Both statements sort of ring true, don't they?

There are those in the mainstream media who don't think outdoor writers are real journalists, and in some ways they're right. Outdoor writing has always been as gonzo as Hunter Thompson: the stories are subjective, often written in the first person with the writer as a character making value judgments right and left.

Those of us who write about fishing are not exactly on a perpetual vacation, as some seem to think, but it's also true that the crappiest jobs in journalism are not in outdoor writing. The worst is what they call "grave digging." That's where someone has just lost three kids in a train wreck and you go to their house and ask, "So how do you feel?"

In case there's any doubt, the proper response to that is one I heard years ago, namely, "Get the hell off my front porch, you vulture!"

So maybe some of us are more like freelance essayists than genuine reporters, but the fact is, even an outdoor writer bears some responsibility for the stories he writes, especially when he knows damn well what the consequences are likely to be.

As far as readers go, the vast majority I've talked to over the years understand the nature of the dilemma, even if they don't always approve of how you handle it. Among the rest there are those who'll get on you if you spill the beans and others who'll get on you just as hard if you don't. When you look at it that way, you're a bastard whether you tell or not, so if there's any question at all, you might as well keep your trap shut and be able to look at yourself in the mirror. After all, fishing has a long and honorable tradition of secrecy.

In the end, you try to write stories that will be accurate,

informative and entertaining, but that will also do no harm, while at the same time avoiding cuteness and arrogance. That's a big order, and when you're going through a magazine and come on a good story that seems to have an aura of vagueness about it or a slightly weird angle (you know, that long monologue on caddis hatches with the names of a few rivers tossed in almost too offhandedly), you've probably stumbled upon a writer who's trying to negotiate that dangerously thin line between honesty and betrayal.

When the famous outdoor writer called about that river in Canada, we talked for quite a while—on his dime—about some of the things I've mentioned here and some other things, too. We also decided it was probably time we went fishing together and discussed that a little.

He didn't come right out and ask me not to write about the river—he was too smart and too diplomatic for that. He also didn't exactly point out that he'd fished the thing for years but had never written about it himself—at least not so you could recognize it—but I did come away from the conversation with that in mind.

Just before we hung up he said he really just called to say hi, and that he knew I'd do whatever I thought was right.

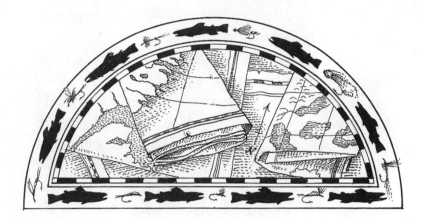

Chapter 17

Where to Fish

A.K. and I just decided, after surprisingly little discussion, not to go back to Labrador next season. We've been there three times in the past three years and have now spent a total of a month fishing the lakes and channels in the Minipi River drainage. On the last trip we spent two weeks there, which was just long enough to get an honest feel for the place, to get a few good breaks from the weird weather, to let one hatch peter out and another begin, to be able to have a slow day now and then without panicking and, well, you know.

We agreed at the outset that two weeks would be better than the regulation six and a half days in camp, but as the end of it approached we began to see that a month would have been even better. It's possible to catch enough fish in two weeks (or even one), but it may not be possible to get comfortably sunk in the place or to finally stop hearing what A.K. calls "the high-pitched whine of civilization," even when the place is a hundred kilometers from the nearest road.

For me at least, that's usually the story at the end of a trip: However long I've stayed, however good the fishing has been, when the Twin Otter comes to take me home, my first impulse is to hide in the forest until it leaves without me.

I don't know how long I'd have to stay in a great fishing spot before I was actually good and ready to go home. I guess the length of time would vary with the place, but I also think there'd be a kind of natural logic to it. In Labrador, for instance, you'd eventually see winter approaching and want to get the hell out in no uncertain terms. A friend of mine was stationed in Labrador over the winter when he was in the military. He said it was the only time in his life he ever seriously considered suicide.

Anyway, by now we've gotten to know some of the guides up there—Howard, Dorman, the brothers Ray and Randy—we've learned some local tricks, caught more trophy-sized brook trout than any two fishermen have a right to and have grasped the whole thing firmly enough that it's made us better fishermen—or at least fishermen with better stories.

Like this one: A sport from the States gets off the plane at the camp, takes one of the guides aside and whispers, "There's a hundred bucks in it for you if you can get me into a five-pound brook trout."

The guide says, "Five-pounders are free. How 'bout a seven-pounder?"

In the end, we came *that close* to becoming regulars: those gentle souls who will book the same week at the same camp every year in perpetuity—until either they die or the money runs out—and who fish there with the patient acceptance of those who have left their restlessness behind. But when I asked A.K. how he felt about going back again next year, he understood just from the question that I was thinking, Maybe not.

He said, "Yeah, I know what you mean," and then asked rhetorically, "How many five-pound brook trout does a guy have to catch anyway?"

He had a point. Once you lose track, it means you've caught plenty—maybe even too many.

We've never actually talked about this, but as I look back over the years we've fished together, it seems like A.K. and I will work new water until we either learn something definitive or finally have that day or week that's so good anything better would begin to belittle the game.

Then we start thinking about moving on to a new place with new fish, and we're not unaware of the dangers in that. I mean, fishing is a matter of timing in a changeable universe, and although it's doubtful that we'll go back to Labrador in five or six years to find a shopping center on the banks of Big Hairy Lake, it's also doubtful that it will be exactly as we remember it. And having once broken the rhythm of the yearly trip, it's possible we'll never go back at all.

Maybe that's as it should be. After all, the one thing you can almost never do in sport (or art or love for that matter) is repeat a brilliant performance. Taken together, lots of trips will sharpen your skills and deepen your patience, but in a practical way, all any single one can do for you is make you a fisherman with a longer past.

Luckily, we've been saved from being perpetual tourists by our home water. We have decades in on some streams and rivers here in Colorado; some famous, some close to unknown outside the county. We've fished these things in good seasons and bad ones, high and low water, seen them change in natural and unnatural ways (sometimes for the better and sometimes not) and paid our dues in full for the great days.

That's what I know I'm missing when I drop in someplace for a week or two during the best fishing of the season. It can be glorious, but in the long run I like the perspective of, say, fishing for bluegills for an extra three weeks in the spring because the neighborhood river, which is supposed to be boiling with Blue-Winged

Olives, is muddy and cold from an unusually high runoff. And then, half a year later, hitting that day in late November or December when the last of the mayflies are finally gone. Not wanting to end the season dredging a favorite river with nymphs and sinkers, my friends and I will wander around in the cold looking for one last dumb fish that will take a dry fly against the odds, maybe getting wistful enough to begin remembering the kind of things we overheard at funerals as children, things like "She's not really dead, honey, she's just going to sleep for a long time now."

I take some comfort in that because, after all, it's truer of the river than it was of Grandma.

We've even stumbled into the quicksand of environmental politics that can be found around trout streams, and at least twice now we've been on what you could call the winning side. In one case the victory was so vague and technical we didn't even feel like celebrating, but never mind. The bad guys were dealt a setback, so it still counts.

It's all amounted to an education. We've learned a lot about fly-fishing and even a thing or two about politics: like, for instance, that even when you're more or less victorious, you still feel like you should take a shower and burn your clothes; that within days of being elected, even a halfway decent politician will develop a fear of democracy; and that the only thing separating a whiner from a spiritual warrior is motive.

We've also encountered some of the hazards of being a

local, most notably the temptation to dispense what could be taken as wisdom if the victim didn't know any better: the same impulse that causes your typical old-timer to point at an American goldfinch and say with authority, "Now, that there is a wild canary."

Fly-fishing has always had its river sages, those people who spend almost all their fishing lives on a single drainage, naming pools, developing fly patterns and maybe even producing one of those rare and wonderful books that are written for no other reason than that the author had something to say.

The lesson there is, it can take a lifetime's worth of attention to learn even half the secrets of a good river, and in our quieter moments that's all a lot of us want for ourselves: something modest but fine. On the other hand, fly-fishers have always had that wanderlust: the irresistible urge to travel a thousand miles, *find* the guy who's spent a lifetime learning the river and hire him as a guide for a couple of days.

A.K. and I have been on a lot of trips together, and if we've been jointly searching for something I don't think I could tell you what it was, although when we travel any distance we do almost always end up in a place where some kind of trout are known to rise to some kind of dry fly, and that probably means something. Big trout are a nice touch, but we've gone to plenty of places where the fish were no better than pan-sized because the streams were new and pretty and because we think all little trickles with trout in them are homes away from home.

One trip is enough for some places, but others draw us back, and I'm glad to say that not all the spots we make second, third and fourth trips to have the biggest or the most fish. I can't say exactly what makes a place click for either of us, and I guess asking why a fisherman falls for one stream and not another is like asking why he married this person instead of that one: it's inexplicable and probably none of your business anyway.

I guess I'd have to say a lot of the fishing A.K. and I do is a little promiscuous, which, as everyone knows, can be dangerous but nonetheless has its charms. But we do have one thing in common with those faithful regulars who migrate back to the same lodge every season. I think we've finally given up on the idea of the fishing trip of a lifetime and now see each expedition as just part of a lifetime of fishing trips.

The ground rules between us are unspoken but fairly simple: If it has to do with trout, A.K. is usually on board. Grayling will work for him too, and, although we've never done it together, salmon would be okay. Bass and panfish are acceptable as long as they don't involve more than an hour's drive. Beyond that, he tends to be skeptical at best. In the past, when I've suggested something like Guadalupe bass in Texas, longnose gar in Kansas or the carp tournament in Fort Smith, Montana, he's said, "Gee, that sounds like fun. Call me when you get back and tell me all about it."

It's not that A.K. is a snob exactly, it's more that he just knows what he likes, and I appreciate that. My tastes are a little more eclectic than his, but I guess that's why most of us end up with more than one friend. (I have friends who've been known to shoot carp through thin ice with shotguns, so there's lots of leeway there.) And anyway, in the long run, a trip is more about who you're traveling with than where you go or what you're after.

Realizing we're not going back to Labrador has left a kind of vacuum that A.K. and I will eventually fill with another place we'd like to fish. I don't know how we do that, I just know it always happens, sometimes over the telephone, more often on the drives to and from local rivers. The talk begins and spreads in widening circles, and eventually a hole opens up in the fabric of things that must be plugged with rods, duffel bags, new fly patterns and either gas money or plane tickets. It's clear we'll end up fishing in some strange new place, the only question is, where?

That sounds like compulsive behavior and maybe it is. It's true that there are fly-fishers who go at it almost angrily, as if they were fighting the Trout Wars, and it's also true that the world as it is now makes us all at least a little bit crazy. Still, A.K. and I allow ourselves a happier diagnosis than that. There are thousands of places to fish and we, after all, are fishermen. Therefore, life is good.

Chapter 18

Stage Two

IALWAYS start feeling a kind of restlessness in the fall. Ten years ago I'd have called it desperation, and I guess ten years ago that's what it was. The only difference now is, although I still know that over the next couple of months the fishing will dwindle from the best of the season to a few meager possibilities, I no longer think that if I try real hard I can catch every trout in the state before that happens.

I see the same kind of thing in the people I spend a lot of time fishing with. We're all firmly in middle age now—and in some cases that assumes a life span of 130—but we're still in what bamboo rod maker John Bradford calls "Stage Two."

Stage One, John says, is when you fish from dawn till dusk without a break, get quickly drunk on something cheap, spend the night wrapped in a wet blanket, eat cold beans from the can and don't even notice, let alone care. At the end of a Stage One trip, you'll drive all night and show up at work without sleep and half an hour late. You won't care about that, either, although your boss might. But if he fires you, it only means you have more time to fish.

Stage Two is when you invest in a tent, a sleeping bag and a folding chair and start cooking your food and maybe even brushing your teeth every few days. You still camp out, but your camps are a little more luxurious. You still fish hard, but you pace yourself a little more reasonably.

Stage Three, where John claims he is now, is when you say the hell with it and just rent a cabin.

John told us this last September over dinner at Andrea's Café in Lyons, Colorado. He was passing through, heading back home to Texas after a week of fishing somewhere in Wyoming. He showed us a lot of snapshots of big brown and rainbow trout and stretches of a pretty stream meandering through rolling, sage-covered hills, but when we asked him exactly where this was, "somewhere in Wyoming" is all we could get out of him. Presumably it was someplace where you could rent a cabin.

I bought one of John's bamboo fly rods that day: a beautiful little 7½-foot, 5-weight built, "more or less" he said, on a Payne taper. Being a rod maker, he just naturally happened to have a few of his new rods with him on the trip, and he casually asked Mike Clark and me to cast them and tell him what we thought. It was the softest sales pitch I've ever seen.

The next day John headed back to Texas and Mike, A.K., Ed and I left for a week on the Frying Pan River. We drove over in three separate trucks because we thought we might have to leave at separate times—and because we can no longer get all our camping stuff into a single pickup. We met at our friend Roy Palm's place, where we always set up our elaborate camp: two full camp kitchens hung from adjoining narrow-leaf cottonwood trees with a tarp stretched over them to keep the rain and snow off, plus tents, numerous coolers and food boxes, folding camp table, lanterns, lawn chairs, tarp-covered woodpile: the full Stage Two catastrophe.

Roy says it always looks like a band of Gypsies has moved in, and it's true enough that we all used to make more spartan camps, but then there's something to be said for a little warmth and comfort when you're settling in to fish one spot for a week.

The fishing on the Pan is always entirely recognizable, but it's also never quite the same two years in a row, which I guess is why you keep going back to a favorite place: as much for the small surprises as for the predictability of it. That year the size-18 to -22 Blue-Winged Olive hatches were heavy and the size-16 Sulphurs were pretty sparse, but for some reason it was the Sulphurs the fish wanted. If we were working an Olive hatch—getting a few strikes here and there—and saw so much as a single Sulphur float by, we'd switch to that fly pattern and start to really hammer them.

Of course "that pattern" started the usual debate. Ed, A.K. and I caught some of the bugs and agonized over their exact size and color. A parachute dry fly tied on a size-16 hook worked okay, but Ed and I thought maybe a long-shanked 16 (what amounts to an old English-style size 15) would be a little closer to precisely the right body length.

A.K. said the color of the natural mayfly was a sort of yellowish, pinkish pale bronze and started rummaging through his huge fly-tying travel kit looking for the right rooster neck and the precise shade of dubbing. Of course I could clearly see that it was a yellowish, pinkish, *rusty* bronze.

Naturally, all three of us used our own flies and caught fish, while Mike caught just as many on a #14 Olive Quill, even though we all carefully explained to him that it was the wrong size and the wrong color.

True to form for the Pan, the best fishing was in the lousiest weather. The first day was gray, cool and a little drizzly off and on. The hatches were good, the fish were up, and we all did well.

Stage Two

The second morning we woke up to a skiff of snow on the ground and a glaze of ice on the tents. The day was dark, chilly and dank with cold rain switching off with wet snow and a penetrating breeze. We cooked and ate breakfast bundled in down vests and wool Miller mitts and added rain slickers to that when we went fishing.

The hatches started early and the trout moved up into the fast water to gorge on bugs. The fish were seriously on: hungry, eager, maybe even a little desperate. We'd learned the trick with the Sulphur mayflies the day before and we pretty much had it wired. If we could get a decent drift over a rising trout, we could pretty much catch him, or at least get a solid strike. It was that perfect balance you're always looking for: The fishing was easy enough that you could catch lots of trout, but still just hard enough to tell yourself you sort of had to know what you were doing, in conditions miserable enough to make you feel like you deserved every fish just for having the guts to stay out.

About midafternoon Ed and A.K. got cold and went over to Roy's cabin to warm up. Mike followed sometime later; after countless fish, his Olive Quill finally fell apart, and he said his hands were too numb to tie on a fresh one. I was doing so well I stayed out a while longer.

I almost gave it up half an hour later when I hooked a fly in a bush on the far bank, broke it off on purpose and ended up losing two-thirds of my hand-tied leader. I was wet and cold, my hands were numb, I'd lost track of the fish I'd caught. I could clearly picture Roy's warm, dry kitchen filled with people whose company I enjoy. On the other hand, the trout were still rising. I asked myself, What would John Wayne do in a situation like this?

I went back to camp, got out of the rain under the tarp and started a pot of coffee. My fingers warmed up enough over the propane burner that I could tie knots, so I rebuilt the leader and tied on a fresh #16 Sulphur Parachute. That took a while, and by the time I was finished I'd bolted two big cups of hot boiled Colombian and was either warmed up nicely or too buzzed to realize I was still cold.

I guess I lasted another hour or so, getting more and more miserable because I was cold and wet, but also more and more delighted because I was catching lots of trout on a beautiful new bamboo fly rod. The emotional ambiguity of it all was enough to make me want to laugh insanely, but I resisted the impulse even though I was alone. I know from experience that insane laughter can be difficult to stop.

When I finally dragged myself over to the cabin to get warm, I was so soaked I had to stop on the back porch and shake myself off like a dog. When I walked in, A.K. glanced up from his drink with a questioning look, apparently read the answer in my face and said, "You son of a bitch, you whacked 'em, didn't you?"

I modestly allowed as how I had, in fact, whacked a few. Then Roy patted me on the shoulder and said, "Well, I always said you were a tough old bird."

I remember feeling good about that—except maybe for the "old bird" part.

Later that night, as we huddled around the fire in damp lawn chairs, putting off going to bed as long as we could because of the ice-cold sleeping bags, I began to think that maybe renting a cabin wasn't such a bad idea after all, at least late in the season when it starts to get nasty out. This would be how Stage Three begins: with just the slightest weakening of resolve at the end of a glorious but miserable day of fishing.

And then I realized I'd forgotten to ask John if there's a Stage Four.

Chapter 19

Big Thompson

M^Y friend Mike Price caught me at a weak moment and convinced me to go fishing. I'd only been back from a trip through Alberta and British Columbia for a day, just long enough to take a shower, get half unpacked and put in an exhausted night's sleep. I was still in that decompression zone where I'd be living out of the duffel bag for another two or three days, not quite ready to be back. I knew there were a few chores I was supposed to take care of, but I hadn't gotten around to figuring out what they were, let alone putting them in order and starting at the beginning.

I'd given Mike the short version of the trip over lunch at the café: rivers fished, biggest trout caught, the two or three funniest things the guide said. I told him how we'd gone to a pretty little stream with big cutthroats in it that the guide called Beaver Creek. Back at the motel that night I looked it up on the map and found that the guide had given the creek a phony name in case we blabbed about it. The real Beaver Creek was somewhere else entirely, and probably full of suckers.

Then Mike asked, "So what are you doing this afternoon?"

"I don't know," I said, "but I should do *something.*"

"Let's go fish the Thompson."

I really did have some work to do, and I'd just gotten back from a good week of fishing, which usually puts me in the kind of calm but energized mood that lets me get a lot done. But then this was mid-August, the beginning of the best eight weeks of trout fishing in the whole year, and one good trip seemed to have just barely scratched the surface.

Then too, sometimes the only way to fight post-fishing-trip depression is to go fishing again.

I said, "Okay."

We got on the water at about 3:30 and split up along a good stretch. Mike said he'd really whacked them there on caddis the day before, so I purposefully didn't tie on a caddis pattern. It's hard enough to repeat your own performance, let alone someone else's.

I hiked downstream a few hundred yards and got in at the bottom of a nice, long, riffly pool with some soft water along the left bank where two trout were rising. I couldn't see anything on the surface, but there were a few mayflies in the air: small, pale ones and larger, dark ones that I guessed to be Pale Morning Duns and Flavilineas.

All I'd brought was a spool of 5X tippet and the small stream box, so I didn't have a lot of flies to choose from, but I did have a couple of size-14 Hares Ear Parachutes that had worked well as a Flavilinea just two days before in British Columbia. I confidently tied one on, and in five casts I'd put down both fish.

Okay. That happens. No need to panic. I fished the water with the same fly for a few more minutes, then changed to a small hopper and worked my way upstream through some pocket water, figuring a grasshopper should work on a warm summer afternoon. One good trout flashed the fly, but he didn't eat it.

There was another long pool around the bend where a handful of trout were rising to a sparse Pale Morning Dun hatch. The flies were between a size 18 and a 20. I don't usually carry anything like that in the small-stream box, but I looked anyway, and sure enough, stuck down in a corner was a single beat-up PMD parachute, size 18. I'd probably left it there during a hasty fly change on the Old Man River in Alberta the week before, figuring I'd put it back where it belonged later.

I tied the fly on, greased it up and over the next half hour showed it to every rising fish in the pool. A few looked at it and refused it. Two little dumb ones actually tried to eat it, but I missed them both.

I sat on a rock for a few minutes wishing I had my full vest instead of just that one small box stuffed in a hip pocket. If I'd had my PMD dries, cripples, emergers and floating nymphs in two or three sizes, I'd have caught a few fish. No doubt about it.

Then I wrote it off as one of those days when I went fishing just to go fishing, not caring whether I caught anything or not—until I was on the water.

Mike did well that day, but I went for a long time without catching a fish. In the early evening we found some trout rising to a hatch of little size-20 yellow caddis flies. My smallest caddis was a size 16 and the fish wouldn't buy it, but I fished that lonesome, ragged #18 PMD—which was sort of the right color and only a size too big—and fooled a couple of little ones in the fast water.

Then, as dusk came on, there was a good Pale Morning Dun spinner fall, and for half an hour or so, the trout bought the #18 parachute as an early spinner and I caught four, including a good-sized brown.

Something to think about: If you fish the wrong fly long and hard enough, it will sooner or later become the *right* fly.

It was a little embarrassing to be caught short like that, but it worked out okay in the end, and I like to think it was a forgivable mistake. In recent years the Thompson has gotten a long catch-and-release stretch and has attracted the attention of a lot of fly-fishers, so the fishing has gotten a little technical, but my mental picture of the river predates all that by quite a few years.

I guess I just don't fish it enough. The Thompson is only a half hour's drive from home, and I do usually manage to get up there once or twice every year, usually when someone else suggests it. It's a perfectly good trout stream—better than it used to be, actually—but I've never really gotten into it. I say it's because there are too many fishermen and because the traffic on the highway that runs along it is too loud, but I have to admit that there's always room for me to fish and that when the trout are biting I don't hear the cars.

I think the real reason I don't fish it much is, I've always suspected I was supposed to die there a little over twenty years ago.

I don't remember every time I've fished the Thompson, but I know for sure I was there with a friend on July 31, 1976. The fishing was poor that day and about midafternoon my partner said he knew of a stream on a ranch just over the border in Wyoming that a guy would probably let us on. He said we could be there in less than three hours, in time for the evening rise.

I said, "What the hell, it couldn't be any worse than this."

We were in Wyoming for a couple of days. I don't recall much about the fishing except that we caught some trout, but when we stopped for gas on the way out I vividly remember glancing at the newspaper machine. The headline said something about the ongoing cleanup and rescue efforts after the deadly Big Thompson flood. I sprang for the quarter and bought a paper. Or maybe it was still just a dime then.

When we'd left the Thompson River, the day had been hot and bright (that's why the fishing was off), but by late afternoon an "intense, heavy, slow-moving thunderstorm" had built up. The upslope effect along the front range had pushed it back into the headwaters of the Thompson, where it had dropped an incredible 10 inches of rain in a few hours. The resulting flash flood in the Thompson Canyon that evening killed 148 people.

If we'd stayed, we'd have certainly been on the water then. The dark sky and humid air would have brought on a good evening hatch and we'd have eagerly stayed out in the weather. It's what you wait for on a hot summer day in the mountains: the purple sky, the cool breeze, the gut feeling that something really memorable is about to happen. It was never mentioned in the accounts of the survivors, but I've always thought that just ahead of that awful wall of water there were trout rising in every pool.

It had been three days since the flood. All anyone knew about my friend and me was that we'd gone up there to fish that day and hadn't been heard from since.

My partner was busy pumping gas, peeing and getting coffee for the road, so I was left alone with the news for a few minutes. It must have been a chilling moment, but what I remember now is the realization that this was my chance to vanish completely, become someone else, start fresh. No one would suspect. For all I knew, my friend and I were already listed among the dead, many of whom, the newspaper said, would probably never be found.

It was tempting. Unfortunately I was a young, carefree hippie in those days with nothing much to leave behind but nothing much to run away from either. It was just an idle thought. I showed my friend the paper. We found phones, called our respective roommates and said, "We're alive. Don't call our mothers. Don't come on to our girl-friends. Don't sell our stuff."

Looking at the Thompson now, you'd never know any of it happened. There are summer cabins, a few tourist joints, a nice-looking little trout river flowing beside a two-lane paved road with a fair number of fly-fishers on it most days. Some of the fishermen are newcomers who haven't heard about the flood, others are too young to re-member much about it. To them the signs saying "Climb to Safety in Case of a Flash Flood" probably just seem like ordinary bureaucratic redundancy. I know the pools are all different now, but I don't think I could take you up there and tell you how it used to look. Twenty years is a long time.

So I still fish the stream now and then—once or twice a year, usually at the suggestion of someone else. It's a lot harder to fish than it used to be (and I think I'll remember that next time), but the trout are also bigger. That seems like as close to breaking even as you're likely to get these days.

I have nothing against the river—it doesn't haunt me or anything—but I guess it still nags at me a little bit. I didn't vanish there in 1976 and go off to start a new life, and I'm not sorry about that. It's just that sometimes I wonder if I'll ever get another chance.

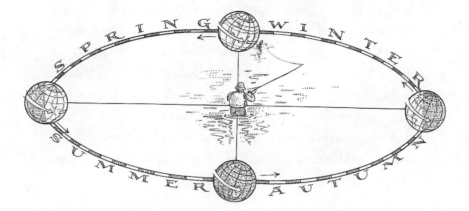

Chapter 20

The Lake

WE do fly-fish all winter here in Colorado, if only because there's no closed season, there's usually some water open somewhere, and we either have such a firm hold on reality we can take the bad with the good or such a loose grip we can't tell the difference.

Usually the fishing is okay. By that I mean you fish your brains out, and more often than not, actually hook a trout or two. There are rare days when you do better than that, and about as many more when you do worse. It's fishing: There's fresh air, open country, good talk, pots of coffee over a twig fire, but along about March it begins to wear thin. You swear that once the trout start rising you'll never fish a nymph again—which is understood to mean not for a couple of weeks, at least. You may not put it in so many words, but you've temporarily abandoned the idea that fly-fishing is an art form, a philosophical pursuit that teaches stillness and patience. You want to catch some goddamned fish.

But then fly-fishing can be a game of last-minute saves, and you know that the best winter fishing is sometimes within sight of the vernal equinox, though still on the back side, so it counts—if it still really matters.

There was exactly a week of winter left when a guy from a pay-to-fish place up north of here called to say the ice was off the big lake, the trout were rising, and no one had fished it yet that year. The call interrupted me while I was tying a dry fly, which I took to be a sign.

"What are they rising *to?*" I asked.

"Nothing," he said. "There's nothing on the water."

"Of course there's something on the water," I said. "Otherwise they wouldn't be rising, right?"

"Yeah, I guess."

I've always appreciated this guy's attitude. You pay him a few bucks to fish, and there *are* trout in the lake, but he has chores to do, so the rest of it is up to you—as it should be.

The Lake

Some friends and I have fished this lake off and on for several seasons now, and we've decided it's best from late March into April, depending on the weather. It's spring-fed, but it's also an open lowland pond, just barely in the foothills, so in summer it gets warm enough and bright enough to put the fish off through most of the day. Also, the paying fishermen really start to show up in the warm days of late April, and by the time the Callibaetis mayflies are on in a big way, the fish have already been pounded a little too hard, if not always skillfully.

So we fish it early. Sometimes *too* early, but when it works we feel like we've pulled a successful raid: slipping in, hanging some hogs and then slipping back out while the sissies who wait for fairy-tale spring, with its flowers and meadowlarks, are still at home moping.

When it occasionally *doesn't* work, it's another day in the life to be made the best of. Art form. Stillness. Patience.

I think weather is crucial, especially at this shifty time of year and especially on ponds and lakes. You want to have had some sunny, warmish weather to get the bugs and the trout moving, but when you actually fish you want it to be during a relapse, under a low-pressure front with overcast skies, chilly air, a little breeze to put a chop on the water and, ideally, either cold rain or wet snow.

There are lots of theories about why that is, and I don't know if any of them is right. All I know is, many if not most of the best days of trout fishing I've ever had were downright miserable to be out in.

———

We told the guy at the lake there'd be four of us—me, Mike, Pat and Pat's cousin, Tim, who was visiting from the Upper Peninsula of Michigan. We were several days into a fine March thaw with bright sun and temperatures in the 60s, but we'd scheduled the lake for the day after the next snowstorm was supposed to hit. Tim was game, but he seemed less than thrilled, possibly because of his job.

Mike had asked him what he did in the U.P.

"I drive a snowplow," Tim said.

Mike, always the diplomat, said, "Aw, jeez!"

But Tim was, above all else, a recognizable fisherman, and so he really *was* game, and not at all grim about it, either. I've noticed that many of the people I've really enjoyed fishing with over the years have turned out to be sturdy peasant stock from Michigan. I don't know what it is about the anglers from that state, but you can spot it: some kind of casual facility with difficulty, or the belief that suffering is the only promise life keeps, so that when things go even a little bit right, it's like a gift.

Then again, maybe it's as simple as a genetic lack of pretension. Pat is also originally from the U.P. You could describe him, accurately, as a talented and successful musician, good fly-fisherman and connoisseur of fine tackle, but on the water he somehow manages to look and act like a regular doof with a slightly twisted, rural sense of humor. There's a photograph of him in the album in

Mike's rod shop holding a 25-inch rainbow from the lake. He's dressed in warm, bulky work clothes with his hat pulled down far enough to make his ears stick out, and he looks like he's never seen a trout before, let alone a big one. Mike and I have titled the photo, "You can take the boy out of the U.P., but you can't take da Yooper out of da boy, ey?"

We lucked out at the lake. The weather had turned really ugly, as predicted—there was a low, gray sky, wet, spitting snow, chilly breeze—but it wasn't quite ugly enough for line to freeze in the guides of a fly rod. It was perfect. When the guy came by to collect our money he said, "Boy, every time you guys come up here it's shitty weather." He doesn't seem to realize we plan it that way.

When we pulled up to the lake at about 7:30, skidding wildly in the slimy gumbo of the dirt road, two bald eagles and a golden flushed from the cottonwood trees along the west bank of the lake and a herd of twenty or thirty horses, still unused to fishermen, trotted over thinking we were ranch hands with a load of feed. (One thing that saves this place from being too posh is that this part of it is still a working ranch, so there's always the smell of manure to remind you who and where you are.)

We rigged up, slogged over to the pond through the mud and horse turds and found a few fish boiling sporadically here and there. Not a classic rise of trout, but enough to make you want to fish an unweighted, if not properly "dry" fly. I don't know what everyone started with, but I tied on a favorite biot midge emerger, a size 20, and I know Mike started with a bead-head Pheasant Tail, because he knows I don't like them and so loves to catch fish on them when I'm around.

As usual, the trout were concentrated in a trough that lies along the west bank and over into a shallow, sloping flat that runs around to the east. It was one of those situations where you'd cast to a fish if one was boiling in range, and otherwise just fish the water hoping to pick up a cruiser. Now and then you'd have to stop and warm your hands inside your waders.

We caught fish more or less steadily all morning. I don't know how many, but we'd lost track before noon, and that qualifies as enough. Each of us used his own version of a midge emerger: a little fly that's fished under the surface but close enough to the top that you can see the boil when a fish takes it. That had to be it, even though, just as the guy had said, there didn't seem to be anything on the water.

The trout in this lake are managed for size, and most are in the 16- to 18-inch class, with a few up to, say, 20 to 22, plus the odd hog like the one in Pat's photo. Most are rainbows, although in seasons past we'd hung a few cutthroats there.

About half the trout I caught that day were a little on the thin side; not sickly or anything, and not really disappointing either, just spawned out. But then the other half either hadn't spawned yet or weren't about to, so they were fat and strong. Pat had one trout, maybe 17 inches long, that took him into his backing. I got two that were both about 22 inches long. One came in like a tired puppy, the other weighed about half a pound more and fought me for a good five minutes, making me worry about the tippet-to-fly knot I hadn't bothered to re-tie after the last big fish.

Things slowed down seriously an hour or so after lunch, and we were all getting pretty cold, so we started a fire, laid out our wet Miller mitts to dry and put on a big pot of coffee. Most of the wet snow had melted down on the floor of the little valley, but it still clung to the hillsides, which looked higher than they really were, being so close to the low clouds.

The delicious aroma of boiling coffee canceled out the stink of burning cottonwood—not the most pleasant-smelling of firewoods—and the toasting wet wool gloves to produce a workmanlike, high plains camp smell. Out on the far side of the valley, hundreds of crows were wheeling over the stubble in that leaves-blowing-in-the-wind maneuver they do. They were chattering like feeding geese, only more high-pitched. Now and then Canada geese, also unused to fishermen, came over in pairs and honked at us for being on their lake.

We'd seen deer, coyote, fox and raccoon tracks in the mud and something, probably a coon, had sat on an overturned aluminum boat and eaten a dozen crawdad tails, leaving the heads and claws. The few winter-killed trout around the lake had been well pecked by the crows, and you had to figure the eagles had accounted for a few as well. One dead trout lying in a foot of water had been systematically disassembled by something—probably crawdads. There'd been plenty of normal, run-of-the-mill carnage going on, and now and then you'd catch that faint, sweet smell of death in the cold air.

Someone said it sure felt like spring all of a sudden, which was true enough in a place where you often have to tell spring from winter by the condition of the snow. The sere browns of the weeds and the mottled grays of cottonwood bark *did* seem warmer than usual. Probably just in the eye of the beholder, but possibly in some actual way; a quality of the light maybe.

We let the fire burn down and went back out to fish until almost dark. The trout had stopped rising, but now and then one would come to a slowly fished streamer with a sullen curiosity strike that seemed to say, "Now, what the hell is *this?*" I enjoyed that, knowing it would happen less and less as the season wore on and the fish saw more flies. I also enjoyed having the pattern that seemed to work best, a local Woolly Bugger variation called a Fire Butt. I handed them out to everyone and didn't care until much later that I'd have to tie more.

By dusk, Pat and I were sitting on the east bank watching the water, hoping for an evening rise to start but knowing that at that time of year it wasn't likely.

Tim was back near the truck, puttering at something. When I saw the curl of white smoke from the fire pit, I figured he was warming up the leftover coffee, which would be good enough under the circumstances.

Mike was still casting. He believes that on a fishing expedition, one fishes. While the rest of us sat or puttered, he caught two more trout.

In this group of fishermen, it's probably fair to say that Pat and I are the most likely bank sitters. On a day when a fair number of large trout have been caught after a long spell of what we'd euphemistically been calling "slow fishing," we're the ones who'll hunker down late in the day to let the relief sink in. I don't know if that's because we're the first to lose faith or the first to have it restored. Or maybe it was one of those days when we'd gone fishing just to make sure it all still worked, and it did. Sometimes that's all it's about.

So we sat there talking about distance casting and crawdad flies (neither of us had any, but they could work there) and gave Mike clenched-fist salutes when he hooked a fish. Pat told me a joke: What's the difference between a dead skunk by the side of the road and a dead trombone player? The skunk was probably on his way to a gig. Musician humor.

And then we somehow got off into childhood crimes. It turns out that one of us once shaved the family cat and the other painted the dog red. It was a long time ago and neither of us could remember why.

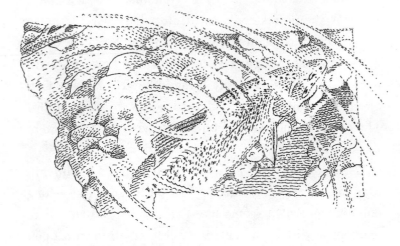

Chapter 21

States of Mind

As corny as it sounds, Montana really *is* a state of mind for fly-fishers, maybe even more so for those who don't live there than for those who do. I say that as a resident of Colorado, which you will find south of Montana, across Wyoming.

Of course Wyoming is a state of mind, too. It's a beautiful place with lots of good fishing, but nonetheless, many

Colorado fly-fishers see it merely as the big thing you have to drive across to reach Montana. For their part, some Wyoming residents call Coloradans "Greenies"—a reference to the color of our license plates as well as of the money we spend on gas and junk food as we drive through the state—and say things like "How many Colorado fishermen does it take to screw in a lightbulb? Three: one to screw in the bulb and two more to 'share in the experience.' "

If I remember right, I first heard about the fly-fishing in Montana in the late sixties or early seventies—long enough ago that it seems like I've always known. There were huge wild trout, they said, not to mention wide open spaces, bison and grizzlies, brutal winters and fewer people living in the entire state than there were in the city of Denver. They made it sound like Alaska, except with pickup trucks instead of float planes.

At the time—back when fly-fishing was a little more provincial than it is now—any stout, heavy fly rod was likely to be the Montana Model and big, bushy dry flies and stonefly nymphs weighing half a pound each were thought of as Montana patterns, even though the same kind of flies could also be used to catch trout in, say, Idaho.

The place functioned as a rite of passage, and fly-fishers in their mid-twenties—like me at the time—would either get a few dollars ahead or have a couple of good days on the Frying Pan or South Platte Rivers here in Colorado and announce that they thought they were "about ready for Montana." By that they would seem to mean the Montana on the map, plus maybe something else that was a little harder to locate.

When I first fly-fished in Montana—with my old friends Koke Winter and A.K.—I was almost disappointed. Sure, the fishing was good: there was more water, the rivers were bigger, the average trout may even have been a little larger than in Colorado, and a size-10 yellow Humpy really did work on the Madison River, but still, it was trout fishing.

I don't mean it was *just* trout fishing, but it was trout fishing, and before I could relax and get into it, I had to stop saying to myself, Well, here you are, by God: *in Montana.* No telling what I'd expected. Enlightenment, maybe, although as any casual student of American Zen is likely to tell you, "When you're finally there, it'll be just like here, man. That's the point."

On the other hand, there were fishermen back home who were not Montana freaks, but they seemed to be overlooking something when they said, "You don't have to drive all the way to Montana for a twenty-inch trout. There are twenty-inchers here in Colorado, and no less of 'em, either." Which was (and is) true enough.

On the surface at least, it seemed to make sense: Why drive twelve or fifteen hours, risking loneliness, fishing-buddy claustrophobia, long stretches of radio silence and speeding tickets to catch what boiled down to the same trout you could catch at home?

Well, in part because those fish *aren't* at home, and if

you discover that the mountains and rivers several hundred miles to the north are a lot like the ones outside your own back door, then you will have begun to grasp the enormousness of your region, just like the Montanans who drive on up to British Columbia to catch the 20-inch trout there and find the place entirely recognizable except for the color of the money.

Actually, I was fishing a river in B.C. a couple of years ago when I met a guy who lived on the banks of a world-famous trout river in Montana. "Why are you here?" I asked.

"Why are *you* here?" he replied. "Why is anybody anywhere?" Both of which are fair questions.

So maybe I got into fishing in Montana just because it was somewhere else. After all, there's a normal progression to these things: After you cut your teeth on your home water, you want to try yourself out someplace famous and fashionable, if only to find out why *it's* famous and the little creek across the street isn't. Later you'll probably begin to hanker for places that are unknown or ignored, and eventually you may stop caring about that one way or the other, although I can't be sure of that.

Anyway, I did get into Montana and have spent a good deal of time there over the last twenty-some years. Eventually I began to get over that weird literary chauvinism we humans have about places like Montana, Texas and Scotland that makes us horror-stricken at the sight of anything that wasn't in the original description supplied by, say, Ernest Schwiebert, Louis L'Amour or Robert Burns.

For instance, the recent infestation of Montana by movie stars is troubling to some. I was fishing a small Montana river a few years ago and I mentioned to a man I know up there that I'd seen some pretty serious hardware parked outside the local roadhouse: Porsches, Mercedeses and Beemers that presumably belonged to the actors and news anchors who had bought ranches in the valley. The man—a ranch foreman who now works for a screenwriter—spat and said, "Yeah, and they serve *cappuccino* now, too."

I understood the problem, but then the only reason that conversation took place was because the screenwriter had let me on his property to fish. That was before the stream-access law, but even under the new rules, it would have meant a ten-mile hike below the high-water line to get on the same water.

Still, cappuccino may not be as harmless as it first appears. Snazzy coffee joints are popping up in some strange places here in Colorado as well as in Montana, and although I'm an old caffeine addict from way back and dearly love the good stuff, I know that gourmet coffee is one of the first two signs that a place is about to go in the crapper. The other sign is a fly shop.

But when it comes right down to it, Montana still has less than its fair share of yuppies and fun-hogs, and the people who were born there (whether they're real cowboys or real estate agents) still have that certain recognizable . . . Well, whatever the hell it is, they still have it.

And many of the new people have the starry-eyed gaze

of those who have chucked it all and moved to Montana, which everyone understands to be completely different from chucking it all and moving to New Jersey. Okay, so maybe there are too many of them, but they won't realize that for another twenty years, if ever. Right now they're just happy and maybe a little lost.

I can relate to that. Back home here in Colorado, I'm as worried as anyone about the exploding population of the West, and there are those who'll tell you I'm one of those old hippie, fly-fishing environmentalist, antigrowth activists. Not everyone means that as a compliment, either, but luckily I live in Boulder County, where there are still small bands of liberals holed up in caves west of town.

I feel okay as a bioregional radical because it's been over a quarter of a century now since I bumbled into Colorado from the Midwest with a few dollars in my pocket and no more possessions than would fit into the back seat of an old Ford Falcon, which I immediately traded in on something with four-wheel drive. If I was part of an influx of counterculture types who crowded out the locals, polluted the regional culture and drove up the property values, I'm really sorry. It was a long time ago. I was young. No one ever asked me what I was doing here, but if they had, I'd have said, "Why is anybody anywhere?"

I was back in Montana just last June, fishing one of the spring creeks around Livingston with a couple of friends. The Pale Morning Dun mayflies weren't in full swing yet, but there were a few scattered, early hatches of them that brought the fish up. Mostly we fished foam beetles with Pheasant Tail Nymph droppers and did well enough. Then at dark we'd go to one of the big, slow pools and cast size-4 Woolly Buggers to the trout that had spooked at tiny dries on 7x tippets in daylight. It's a trick that works more often than not, and I always think, as I'm releasing one of those big trout, There, you're not so damned smart after all, are you? That's as close as you come to victory in a sport with no scoring system.

We fished there for three or four days and always had those big pools to ourselves, because by 7:00 or so most of the sports had left, presumably to pay off their guides and have dinner at one of the fern bars in town. But then my friends and I are of the old school: We cook most of our own meals on a propane stove on the tailgate to save money, and assume that the day you pay $50 for on a spring creek lasts for 24 hours.

One evening when no one felt like cooking, we did drive into town for supper, and the waitress—no spring chicken herself—asked us if we wanted to see the senior citizens' menu. I got flustered and said no. I was forty-eight at the time, seventeen years from official senior citizenship; still apparently young enough to have an attack of vanity. Later, back in camp, Ed said, "You know, if you'd just kept your mouth shut, we'd have saved a few bucks on our burgers."

I remembered that the first time I fished in Montana I got a little bent because someone in a bar called me "kid," the point being that you can't win, or maybe that patience is a virtue. One or the other.

The first time I fished that spring creek, I *was* younger, the rod fee was cheaper, and the place seemed a little more exotic. By now it's almost familiar, as are a few other places where I have favorite pools and know the local fly-shop owner by name, or in some cases, at least knew the *old* owner by name. But then that's part of the romance. If you're a middle-aged fly-fisher living in the American West, having a little history in Montana is pretty much of a requirement.

Except for those spring creeks (in the years when I plan ahead far enough to get my reservation in) I don't fish the really famous Montana rivers much anymore, and when I do I usually hit them at off times—between the major hatches—when, as a guide once told me, "There are fewer rising trout, but more rising trout *per fisherman.*"

I do that in part to avoid the crowds—which really have grown lately in some places—but mostly just to sniff around, see more water and catch some new trout. There was probably a time when I was looking for something different, but now I'm more likely to just enjoy the similarities. Of course no two trout streams are exactly the same, but it's also rare to find one that's unique in a really meaningful way. At the same time, every last one of them is at least worth taking a look at.

Some years ago a friend and I drove up to Montana and hit something like nine lesser-known rivers in eight days. It was a great trip: We saw a lot of country, caught a lot of trout, ran into precious few other fishermen and learned a lot. I could say it was like the old days, but I'm not sure I actually remember the old days. By the time I got to Montana, it had already been splashed all over the fly-fishing magazines, and I think I understood even then that it would no longer be exactly the way the stories described it.

At the end of that trip the plan had been to drive all night and make Colorado by morning, but we ended up crashed in a motel somewhere in Wyoming with bad cases of road burn, and I don't think I've done one quite as crazy as that since. I guess I've finally begun to slow down a little, not because I'm getting tired, but because I've realized that since I've been going to Montana to fish, millions of trout have died of old age before I could catch them and there's not a damned thing I can do about that. However hard you fish, you can only catch trout one at a time.

One evening on the spring creek I got to talking to a young guide who seemed interested that I was night fishing (because he was, too) and also because I'd started fishing that creek not long after he was born—although he was disappointed when I told him the only real difference was that the rod fee was now a lot higher.

We didn't exactly exchange life stories, but I learned that he was a college student working summers as a guide, and I got the impression that he was wondering if he'd finish school and go straight as he'd promised his parents, or chuck it all for the good, hard life in the West that could possibly lead to something more exciting than forty years behind a desk and a comfortable retirement.

He told me he was guiding clients all day, dropping them off in town and then coming back to fish by himself at night—sometimes *all* night—with big deer-hair mouse patterns. He described the monster brown trout he was catching there in the wee hours of the morning, and the insane look in his eyes was only partly from sleep deprivation. The kid clearly had it bad.

I said some wise older fisherman thing like "Yup, those big browns really go nuts for mice," and I almost added, "But look, don't kill yourself; you have a lifetime of fishing ahead of you." But I stopped myself in time. I mean, he was there, he had the big fish wired, and maybe he *didn't* have a lifetime of fishing ahead of him. Who knows?

And anyway, I could remember grown men—old men, I thought then—telling me the same kind of thing when I was his age and thinking, Right, Grandpa, isn't it about time for your nap?

Chapter 22

Jordan River

MY friend Susan and I had gone to northern Michigan for her mother's funeral, but since I've always thought the key to a good life is trying to make the best of things, I brought along a couple of fly rods, just in case.

Of course there was a good chance this would be okay, because this is an old-time fishing family. Irene had died in a nursing home in Colorado in June, and she'd been cremated. The funeral wasn't until August, because that's when the far-flung family traditionally returned to northern Michigan anyway—and they returned then because that's when the big-lake fishing they do for lake trout and salmon starts to get good.

Back when Susan and I had just started seeing each other, August rolled around and she told me she was going back to Michigan to fish with her family. When I left her at the airport I said jokingly, "Bring me back a fish." When I picked her up a week later we were standing at the baggage claim when a crate big enough to hold a railroad tie rolled off the carousel. Susan said, "By the way, there's your fish."

So, as I'd suspected, the family understood the fishing tackle. They approved (more than one relative said Susan's mother would have approved, too), and Susan's cousin Paul even turned me on to a trout-fishing guide on the nearby Jordan River.

His name was Bill Bellinger, and when I called his answering machine it said, "Wild Bill's Guide Service . . . ," which I should have expected. Any fishing guide named Bill will eventually come to be known as *Wild* Bill, either ironically or otherwise.

Anyway, after a little phone tag we connected and set a time, and I got directions to his place. I drove down the next day in Susan's mother's old car: an ancient Chevy Citation that had been left out through too many Michigan winters and looked it. But there were only about 40,000 miles on it, and it actually ran pretty well, although the tires were slightly bald and when you put the automatic transmission into drive it lurched forward a foot as if it couldn't wait to get going.

Bill's directions were good: south on the highway to Such-and-such Road, left toward the river, cabin on the left with a green drift boat parked out front. He said I couldn't miss it. I could have, actually, but I didn't.

The Jordan is a beautiful small river, immediately recognizable as trout water, but unlike the streams we have here in Colorado. The country in that part of Michigan is flat—or I should say, only slightly tilted—so the stream is slow and lazy, with gentle meanders. It's deep, cool, spring-fed, clear as a bell and sandy-bottomed and, because it doesn't get scoured every spring like a mountain stream, it's jumbled with sweepers and sunken cedar logs that can last a century under water. It was pretty much unwadable: In most places you couldn't get past the maze of snags, and if you did you'd sink past your hat.

The trout streams of this size I'm used to back in the Rocky Mountains are steep and loud, and all but the biggest tree trunks get pushed out in the spring runoff, so the channels are open, the bottoms are mostly clean rock, and you have to wade them gingerly and fish them aggressively. By comparison the Jordan was slow and quiet—in most places the wind and the birdsongs were louder than the current. It was downright pastoral.

The woods around the river were lush and thick: mixed pine, fir, balsam, birch and cedar with tangles of alder, carpets of ferns and unfamiliar wildflowers in the rare clearings. Pileated woodpeckers live there. I never saw one, but I think I heard one. Most woodpeckers go "rat-a-tat-tat," but the big pileated woodpeckers go "thunk," and take inch-long chips out of trees.

So Bill, his landlord and I floated a good long stretch of river in Bill's Ausable River boat. This was a lovely, hand-made wooden craft: 21 feet long, narrow, flat-bottomed and a lot more stable than it looked. The hull was no more than a foot high and with three people in it I don't think it drew more than an inch or two of water.

It's the kind of boat that exhibits the beauty of pure function. That is, in the right hands it does one special-ized job to perfection. Bill threaded it expertly down miles of river using a pole from the stern, and I can only remember one unplanned bump, just a few seconds after the landlord said, "So, Bill, which side of that stump are you gonna go on?"

We caught trout more or less regularly, and they were more or less in the kinds of places where you'd expect them to be. Deep holes and slots above and below logjams were good, and so were dark currents along shady banks and the deep edges of snags. In most places the forest was too tight around the banks and the river too narrow for much of a back cast, so there was a lot of roll casting.

The trout weren't especially big (I was on a weird schedule, and we were not fishing at the best time of day, or for that matter, the best time of year, either), but there were plenty of them and they were happy enough to eat a size-12 or -14 dry fly, even though there were few real bugs on the water. They were mostly browns, with some rainbows and a precious few brook trout, all healthy and brightly colored. Brookies are native there and not all that common, so you get excited about them, even the little ones.

I caught some fish on a St. Vrain Caddis dry fly—a favorite back home—but I got most of them on a local pattern Bill gave me. I forget what he called it, but basically it's a Royal Wulff body with a down wing, tail of elk hair, and palmered grizzly hackle—size 12. I found the thing in my fly box a few days after I got back to Colorado. It was chewed almost beyond recognition.

Considering that I'd gone to Michigan for a funeral, I'd already gotten in quite a bit of fishing. The actual morning of the funeral I went out on Lake Michigan with three of Susan's cousins, Paul, Roger and Parris.

I'd been hearing about Parris for years. He's fished Lake Michigan all his life—in the family tradition—and has owned three boats called *Fisker* (Norwegian for "fisherman"), although one of the earlier ones was also sometimes known as *Das Boot.*

In all the time I was in Charlevoix, anytime someone mentioned Parris they'd immediately add, in the same reverent tones you'll hear in any fishing community, "The guy can really catch fish." The phrase had become a kind of official title, as in "Former president Jimmy Carter." Parris is acknowledged locally as an expert—if not *the* expert—and there are fishermen who'll spot the current incarnation of *Fisker* out on the lake and follow it.

Parris was a welder by trade until recently, when he retired because of injuries to his hands, but since everyone who cares already knows that, his business card reads: "Parris A. Halverson, Fisherman, Gatherer of Game, Military Analyst and Sage."

We picked Parris up at his one-room cabin at 5:30 in the morning and drove to where *Fisker III* was docked on the south arm of Lake Charlevoix. From there we had to motor up the lake a few miles and go through a channel into Lake Michigan.

That took a while, because the lake was socked in with a dense, cold fog. Parris knew the headings, of course, but we puttered along within sight of shore because, as Roger explained, "Parris doesn't trust compasses." This cost valuable fishing time, but no one said anything. Parris seemed a bit hung over, and it had been explained to me earlier that *Fisker* operated on one simple principle: If the captain ain't happy, no one on the boat is happy.

Fisker III is what they call a porcupine boat because of the four to six long rods that stick off the stern like quills. To catch salmon and lake trout in very deep water, you troll down riggers, or "cannonballs." These are large lead weights that are cranked down to the desired depth on winches. The monofilament fishing line is attached to the weight by a clip and the lure trails some distance behind. When a fish strikes, the clip releases the line, the rod tip springs upward, someone grabs the rod from its holder, and the fight begins.

The boat is also equipped with some serious and expensive electronics, the centerpiece of which is a large, real-time color screen that shows the bottom, the depth, the lures and, of course, the fish. Once the lines are rigged, everyone but the skipper stands around drinking coffee and chatting, now and then strolling into the cabin to watch the monitor.

The whole rig is complicated enough that one person can't fish alone.

I'd heard about this—the point where fishing meets the video game—and it always sounded a little too technological for my taste. In fact, Parris and I had spent some time in a café the day before discussing the pros and cons of our own styles of fishing. It was the kind of diplomatic conversation that has taken place thousands of times between thousands of bearded, middle-aged fishermen:

"Nothing against electronics, but . . . "

"Well, nothing against fly-fishing, but . . . "

Among other things, I learned that buying and properly equipping a good porcupine boat makes fly-fishing look cheap.

When it was all said and done, I landed a seven- or eight-pound lake trout hooked in 110 feet of water on a spoon called a Kevorkian—which turned out to be a lot more fun than I'd expected—and we made it back in time for the funeral. As I was walking into the church, feeling hot and strangled in a tie, another one of Susan's countless cousins stopped me, shook my hand solemnly and asked, "Do any good this morning?"

The next afternoon, I borrowed the Citation, and on a tip from yet another cousin, drove down to explore the headwaters of the Jordan. The guy said, "Take a left at the farm-implement yard and then bear right at every fork. There's a bunch of little creeks up in there."

"Up in there" turned out to be the Mackinaw State Forest, and he was right. Several little tributary streams seeped off the low hills to the west and under the road beneath solid little one-lane wooden bridges heading for the Jordan, which I could now and then glimpse through the trees on my left. At first I was a little concerned about the family-heirloom car, because it sat pretty low to the ground on its elderly shocks, but the dirt roads really were dirt, as opposed to the cobbles and boulders I'm used to, so it bottomed out softly and harmlessly.

With nothing better to go on, I picked the creek with the best head of water in it, strung up a rod and hiked upstream. The woods were thick, the banks were boggy, and the creek itself was slow-flowing and choked with snags, like a miniature version of the Jordan.

There were no fish rising, but I tempted up some brown trout to a caddis dry. Most of them were small, a few would have been big enough to kill and eat, and they didn't seem to have that cagey streak fish get after they've been pounded by fishermen. For that matter, there was no trash, no trail, not so much as flattened grass or a broken twig to show anyone had been near the place at all recently.

About a mile or so up in there I came to a nice beaver pond. There were no fish rising there either, but I hunkered down off to the side of the dam, worked the water I could reach with the caddis fly and caught half a dozen chunky little browns.

Then I teetered out on the dam itself so I'd have the back-cast room I'd need to reach the channel at the head of the pound. I put the fly along an undercut and buggered the cast badly. The fly hit the water way too hard and then ripped down through the current, throwing a wake.

It was enough to spook the great big fish that was hiding there. He flashed out into open, shallow water, froze in confusion for a small fraction of a second and then bolted into the depths of a deadfall.

I want to say it was a brown trout no less than 20 inches long, but I guess I can't swear to that. I'd been told that summer-run steelhead come up the Jordan, and if that's true then they'd probably come up the bigger tributaries, too. Still, although I didn't see the fish that well or for all that long, I think I made out buttery-colored sides and black spots in the split second he froze in the clear shallow water in full sun.

Whatever it was, it made me take a step backward in surprise, and I almost fell off the dam. I danced and waved my arms for a while, and by the time I'd gotten my balance back, the memory had already begun to fade.

After that I crossed the dam and slogged up to where I could see the water upstream. I ended up standing in an acre of tightly packed, shoulder-high joe-pye weeds, every last one of them in full, reddish/purple flower, and actually took a minute to stop and think, Jeez, this is kinda pretty.

From that vantage point, the stream above the dam looked fishy and inviting with slicks, bends and under-cuts, but then I began to think maybe I should get back. At times like that—the day between the funeral and the bur-ial—you think you should be around for moral support, even if the most good you can hope to do is not say the wrong thing.

The next morning we buried Irene and walked over to look at the little brook-trout creek that flows through the cemetery, and then there was the trip to the bank to clean out the safe deposit box. Susan was pretty exhausted by then, but her sense of humor seemed okay. Out in the parking lot she said, "Well, no secret fortune in jewels."

My gear was already in the trunk, so I dropped Susan off at a cousin's house and drove down to the Jordan River to meet Bill. It was a pleasant drive in rural country, south from Charlevoix into Antrim County, through the little town of East Jordan, past the farm-implement place again, and then a hand-painted sign in front of a farmhouse that read, "FOR SALE—MAPLE SYRUP, FIREWOOD, RABBITS."

Jordan River

I remember being happy to be out of town, out of the funeral clothes once and for all, floating quietly down a strange new river that still seemed somehow familiar. I guess I was just feeling the relief that rites for the dead are meant to provide for the living. You're supposed to come away feeling that most of what *could* be done *has* been done, so at least that part of the job is finished. The rest of it will have to sink in slowly, over time, but that can be left to itself. In the meantime, there's an old car no one's using and a little trout river just a few miles away.

And Bill himself was sort of a hopeful, heartwarming sight. He was a young guy—I'd say thirty, tops—living in a sweet little cabin in the woods a stone's throw from a trout river with a great, friendly dog named Killian and a fine handmade wooden boat. I got the feeling that he's exactly what he wants to be: a good-natured, competent, river-wise fishing guide. I know that some guides eventually burn out or—for better or worse—move on to other things, but for now at least, the guy probably thinks he's died and gone to heaven.

About the Author

JOHN GIERACH is the author of several previous books, most recently *Another Lousy Day in Paradise*. His work has appeared in *Field & Stream, Fly Fisherman,* and *Fly Rod & Reel,* among other publications. He lives in Lyons, Colorado.